Derek Walcott

THE CARIBBEAN BIOGRAPHY SERIES

The Caribbean Biography Series from the University of the West Indies Press celebrates and memorializes the architects of Caribbean culture. The series aims to introduce general readers to those individuals who have made sterling contributions to the region in their chosen field – literature, the arts, politics, sports – and are the shapers and bearers of Caribbean identity.

Other Titles in This Series
Earl Lovelace, by Funso Aiyejina
Marcus Garvey, by Rupert Lewis

DEREK WALCOTT

Edward Baugh

The University of the West Indies Press
Jamaica • Barbados • Trinidad and Tobago

The University of the West Indies Press
7A Gibraltar Hall Road, Mona
Kingston 7, Jamaica
www.uwipress.com
© 2017, 2018 by Edward Baugh
All rights reserved. Published 2017

Paperback edition published 2018

A catalogue record of this book is
available from the National Library of Jamaica.
ISBN: 978-976-640-645-5 (cloth)
978-976-640-687-5 (paper)
978-976-640-646-2 (Kindle)
978-976-640-647-9 (ePub)

Cover photograph by Abigail Hadeed,
©abigail hadeed |splicett.com
Cover and book design by Robert Harris
Set in Whitman 11.5/15

Printed in the United States of America

CONTENTS

ONE / 1

TWO / 13

THREE / 24

FOUR / 46

FIVE / 67

SIX / 83

NOTES / 97

BIBLIOGRAPHY / 101

ACKNOWLEDGEMENTS / 105

ONE

Derek Walcott has given words of caution for anyone who undertakes his biography. His essay "On Robert Lowell" begins: "Biographies of poets are hard to believe. The moment they are published they become fiction, subject to the same symmetry of plot, incident, dialogue as the novel. The inarticulate wisdom of really knowing another person is not in the broad sweep of that other person's life but in its gestures; and when the biography is about a poet the duty of giving his life a plot makes the poetry the subplot."[1] Later in the essay Walcott writes, with reference to Lowell: "But we have all done awful things, and most biographies that show the frightening side of their subjects have a way of turning us into moral hypocrites" (*Twilight*, 97).

What follows here is written with an awareness of the shadow of Walcott's words looming over it.

Derek Alton Walcott and his twin brother Roderick (Roddy) Aldon Walcott were born in Castries, capital of the island of

St Lucia, on 23 January 1930, to Warwick and Alix Walcott (née Maarlin). Their sister, Pamela, was two years older than they. On 23 April 1931, when the boys were just one year and three months old, Warwick died, after surgery necessitated by mastoiditis. He was thirty-four years old. He had been a civil servant, clerk of the First District Court, and on the day of his death he was to have assumed duties as acting deputy registrar. His wife, Alix, popularly known as Teacher Alix, was the highly regarded head teacher of the Methodist Infant School, which was situated just "round the corner" from the Walcott house on Chaussee Road. She acted on occasion as head teacher of the Methodist Primary School. She never remarried. Her avocation was that of seamstress, and Derek, in chapter 2 of *Another Life*, extols the energy with which she worked at her Singer sewing machine to make ends meet.

To consider Derek Walcott's family background is to recognize the problematics of colour and class in West Indian society and culture, and their cause-effect link with West Indian history. It is to recognize these factors as determining issues in the construction of self that runs through Walcott's poetry, and in his exploration of the "divided" self. Both his grandfathers were white, European, and both his grandmothers coloured, of part-African ancestry. Shabine, protagonist of "The Schooner *Flight*", speaks for the poet, half-tongue-in-cheek, when he says, "I have Dutch, nigger and English in me, / and either I'm nobody or I'm a nation" (*Star-Apple*, 4).

His paternal grandfather was an Englishman, Charles Walcott, who had come to St Lucia from Barbados to manage a sugar estate at Choiseul, where he soon acquired his own estate. Warwick was one of the children he sired by Christiana Wardrope, a local woman from La Fargue, who became his wife. He also fathered children by other women. Derek broached in his poetry the niceties of tension in his idea of his grandfather. In "Veranda" (*The Castaway*) he works through the recognition of the grandfather as representative of the colonizer, to acceptance of his humanity and his role in the making of his grandson. In "The Train" (*Gulf*, 24), as he rides on a train through the English countryside, Walcott asks, "Where was my randy white grandsire from?" He again poignantly voices his mixed feelings and acknowledges, acceptingly, his identification with his grandfather.

Derek's maternal grandfather, whom he never knew, was Johannes van Romondt, a wealthy estate-owner and trader of St Maarten in the Netherlands Antilles. Derek's maternal grandmother was Caroline Maarlin, a domestic worker in the household of Johannes. She and Alix migrated to St Lucia when Alix was a child. Caroline became Mrs Husbands, wife of a Methodist catechist who had come to St Lucia from Guyana. Alix travelled by schooner to St Maarten in her teens, to visit her father, but her mother discouraged her from cultivating that relationship. Alix said that her sewing machine (the Singer that Walcott writes about in *Another Life*?) was a gift from her father.

In *The Prodigal* and *White Egrets*, we look in on Walcott's quest for the grandfather whom he never knew, a quest involving tensions akin to those in his reflections on his English grandfather. In a restaurant in Lausanne, some men remind him of Rembrandt's *Syndics of the Drapers' Guild*. He imagines that one of them could be his grandfather. He imagines

> a syndicate
> in which, far back, a negligible ancestor
> might have been a member, greeting me
> a product of his empire's miscegenation
> in old St Martin.
>
> (*Prodigal*, 16)

In the poem "In Amsterdam", he ponders the idea of affirming his Dutch heritage:

> Silly to think of a heritage when there isn't much,
> though my mother whose surname was Marlin or Van der Mont
> took pride in an ancestry she claimed was Dutch.
> Now here in Amsterdam, her claim starts to mount.
> Legitimate, illegitimate . . . .
>
> (*White Egrets*, 64)

Other aspects of the social context which helped shape Walcott in his childhood and youth had to do with religion and education. He belonged to a Protestant (Methodist) minority in a country that was overwhelmingly Roman Catholic. While this allowed him a certain freedom of expression, it also in some instances subjected his creative work to proscription by Catholic tenets. He was at one and the same time attracted to certain aspects of Catholicism and happy to be outside of it. But the denominational situation did not create social barriers. Walcott's friend, the painter

CHAPTER ONE

Dunstan St Omer, was a devout Roman Catholic. Also Catholic was his first love, Andreuille Alcée, the Anna of *Another Life*. At the time when he fell in love with her, she was a student at St Joseph's Convent school, and Derek designed and painted the set for a play staged at the school.

Walcott's high school, St Mary's College, the only high school for boys at the time, was also Roman Catholic. St Lucia being a British colony, the education system was British, and the school offered an English public school curriculum. History was British imperial history, and the history master, who was also the headmaster, from 1934 to 1946, was the militaristic T.E. Fox Hawes, described in *Another Life* and in "Leaving School". Walcott, when he joined the teaching staff in 1947, right after leaving school, enjoyed a good relationship with Brother Liam, one of the Irish Brothers of the Presentation, who taught mathematics but also wrote poetry and widened the young poet's knowledge of Irish poetry.

Although the Walcott boys never really knew their father, he was ever present in their imaginations, not only as the model of a gentleman held up to them by their mother, but also for his example in the arts. He was a watercolourist: his self-portrait hung on the wall, as did his painting of the coconut walk at Vigie and his reproduction of Millais's *The Gleaners*. The boys thumbed through his book of drawings by Albrecht Dürer, and his books of reproductions by English watercolourists such as Paul Sandby and John Cotman, and paintings by François Boucher and Jean-Honoré Fragonard. No doubt Derek's career as a painter owed something of its beginnings to his father's example.

Warwick had a collection of classical music, and Roddy remembered Alix singing operatic arias "in her off-key soprano".[2] Warwick also wrote poetry and dramatic sketches. He founded the Star Literary Club, which did readings, among themselves, from English literature, and sometimes extracts from Shakespeare. Alix kept the theatrical venture alive after his death. She was often heard reciting Portia's speeches around the house, as well as poems by Wordsworth, Tennyson and Kipling. When Derek had his first slim collection of poems ready for publication, he did not have the money to pay for its printing. He has repeatedly expressed his gratitude to his mother, who gave him the two hundred dollars that enabled him to have 25 *Poems* printed in Trinidad in 1948.

Adult mentor-friends played a part in enhancing Derek's artistic bent. Grace Augustin, a friend of his father's, would invite the boys to spend some of their school-vacation time at her Patience estate, off the road between Castries and Vieux Fort. These forays deepened his knowledge and love of the St Lucian landscape. It was at Patience, when he was fourteen, that, as he records in chapter 7 of his verse-autobiography *Another Life*, he had the visionary experience of losing himself in the light and beauty of the landscape. This possession by the landscape was further deepened by his painting trips around the countryside with his friend Dunstan St Omer, who was to become St Lucia's foremost painter. St Omer is one of the main "characters" in Walcott's *Another Life*, where he is named Gregorias.

Another benefit derived by Derek and Roddy from their visits to the countryside, one which both made a point of recalling, was their hearing of St Lucian folk tales from an unforgettable storyteller, their great-aunt Sidone Wardrope at La Fargue.

For a time, Walcott was not sure whether he wanted to become primarily a poet or a painter. Although he never gave up painting, the acknowledgement that poetry would be his defining commitment no doubt owed something to another mentor-friend, Harold Simmons, who, interestingly enough, was his early painting instructor, and who was St Lucia's foremost painter in his day. In 1950, Walcott and St Omer held a joint exhibition in Castries. In his review of the exhibition (*Bim*, no. 13, December 1950), Simmons forecast that St Omer would come into his own as painter, Walcott as poet.

Simmons was widely read and he allowed young Walcott access to his library. Simmons was a self-made authority on St Lucian culture, and in this regard also played a part in his protégé's creative feeling for the island. Simmons, a highly regarded civil servant, was also not only artist, but historian, folklorist, newspaper editor, botanist, lepidopterist and stamp collector. Walcott's "Letter to a Painter in England" (*In a Green Night*) is his early act of homage to his master, and Simmons became the informing, overarching presence in *Another Life*.

When Walcott's first collection, *25 Poems* (1948), appeared, Simmons recommended it enthusiastically to Frank Collymore, the Barbadian editor of the little magazine *Bim*, a seedbed for the newly bourgeoning West Indian literature. Collymore in turn became Walcott's mentor and friend. Thanks to Collymore's help, Walcott was able to get not only a second edition of *25 Poems*, but also *Epitaph for the Young* printed in Barbados, both in 1949, and then, in 1950, *Henri Christophe*. Also in 1949, Collymore delivered to a meeting of the Literary Society of Barbados the first lecture ever given on Walcott's work. It was published in *Bim* (no. 10, June 1949). In August–September 1949 Walcott visited Barbados for two weeks and stayed for one of the two with the Collymores. The friendship deepened. Between 1949 and 1969, some thirty-eight poems by Walcott appeared in *Bim*.

Collymore was also influential in the widening of Walcott's reputation by way of the British Broadcasting Corporation's *Caribbean Voices* programme. In March 1949, Collymore sent to the programme's producer-editor, Henry Swanzy, a copy of *25 Poems*. On 22 May, the programme broadcast a review of it, by no less a person that the noted British poet Roy Fuller. Fuller spoke encouragingly of the poems, and gave constructive criticism, including that the young poet was too imitative of Dylan Thomas, and might model himself more on the English poets of the 1930s, especially W.H. Auden. This advice seems to have been followed by Walcott in *Poems* (1951), which was also reviewed by Fuller, in the *Caribbean Voices* broadcast for 23 March 1952.

Walcott's *25 Poems* sounds a public, exhortatory note of direct social criticism, a mode which is to become less obvious in his later, more mature poetry. West Indian issues of colour and class are addressed, including middle-class pretension and social climbing. In *Epitaph for the Young* we hear a more self-reflective Walcott, learning, as in *25 Poems*, from leading twentieth-century Western poets, in this instance Ezra Pound and T.S. Eliot, and their experiments in writing the modern long poem. The idea of voyaging/wandering, including towards finding oneself, informs the work, with allusions that reflect Walcott's wide reading. The allusions to the father-son relationship, as relevant to the theme of journey, of being led to understanding, bring into play, for instance, James Joyce (*Portrait of the Artist as a Young Man*), Shakespeare (*Hamlet*), Homer (Ulysses and Telemachus), Walcott and his own father, as well as his surrogate father, Simmons.

Another mentor-friend who was struck by Walcott's poetic promise was James Rodway, a Guyanese who had come to St Lucia to work as an education officer. Like Simmons, he also had a fine collection of books to which he gave Walcott easy access. It was in this way that Walcott had his early knowledge of poets like W.H. Auden and T.S. Eliot. There was also Herman Boxill, Derek's godfather and a teacher at St Mary's College.

Walcott's poetic gift had begun to make its mark in his childhood. When he was ten, his teacher and the headmaster of the primary school were so impressed by a Christmas poem which he had written, that they made him read it to the assembled school. Then, when he was fourteen, he broke into the news, and even into notoriety. On 5 August 1944, the *Voice of St Lucia* carried a poem of his titled "1944". It was forty-four lines of Miltonic blank verse, expressing a pantheistic belief in the presence and power of God as taught by Nature rather than by the mouth of mortal man. Two days later, the paper carried a reply, a poem titled "Reflections", by C. Jesse, FMI, an expatriate priest, historian and popular spokesman for the Roman Catholic Church. Jesse found fault not only with the young poet's style, as being pretentious, but also with his message, as being simply wrong. On 9 August, there was a letter to the editor, from "A Seeker", disagreeing with Father Jesse and encouraging the young poet to persist in his quest.

Then there was theatre. In March 1950, a few friends, including the Walcott twins, met to follow through on an idea that had been suggested to Derek by Maurice Mason. The result was the formation of the St Lucia Arts Guild, which was to prove a path-finding development in the making of West Indian drama. Derek was the guild's first president. Soon after the founding of the guild, Mason left St Lucia to study law in England, and was never involved with the guild thereafter. Also of historic significance with regard to the guild's coming into being was the fact that the first play produced by them, in September 1950, at St Joseph's Convent, was Derek's *Henri Christophe: A Chronicle in Seven Scenes*, directed by the playwright and with costumes by Alix Walcott. This was Derek's first substantial play. It showed him engaging with a Caribbean subject but within a Classical-Shakespearean mould. It portrays Christophe as the tragic hero done in by his overweening ambition, and this in a grand Elizabethan style.

The St Lucia Arts Guild was to stage other early Derek Walcott plays: in 1951, the apprentice pieces *Paolo and Francesca* and *Three Assassins*; then, in December 1954, it was *The Sea at Dauphin*, one of his most enduring plays, at

CHAPTER ONE

the Methodist Infant School. The set was designed by Dunstan St Omer, who also played the role of Hounakin. By this time Walcott had completed his four years of study at the University College of the West Indies in Jamaica (UCWI). It was there that he wrote *The Sea at Dauphin*. In contrast to *Henri Christophe*, with its attention to the once-colonized and enslaved Caribbean black as revolutionary, all-powerful ruler, fit material for the tragic hero, *The Sea at Dauphin* foregrounds the underprivileged black, in the person of Afa the fisherman, struggling against circumstance, including the perils of the sea, to find place and personhood.

Before graduating from St Mary's College in 1947, Derek had been unsuccessful in his bid for the Island Scholarship, based on the results of the London Matriculation examination, which would have taken him to Oxford or Cambridge University. He taught at St Mary's for two years after leaving school, and was then offered a scholarship to the UCWI by the Commonwealth Development and Welfare organization. Granted his commitment to his island, and his dedicating himself to "naming" it in poetry and in painting, he was nevertheless at a point where that commitment might be enhanced by higher education overseas. There was also the possible stimulus from his becoming involved in theatre outside of St Lucia.

To leave St Lucia at this time would also mean leaving behind his first love, Andreuille Alcée, the Anna whom he lyrically evokes in chapter 7 of *Another Life*. He describes the heart-stopping moment of elation when he, a young schoolmaster, passes her on the street, a schoolgirl laughing with her schoolgirl friends. She lived across the Castries harbour, and Walcott recalls being rowed across the harbour to meet her, the memory deepened by his retrospective premonition of their inevitable, permanent separation.

In late September 1950, he boarded a flight from Vigie Airport en route to Jamaica, to become one of the first students in the Faculty of Arts at the UCWI. The poignancy of that moment of departure is evoked in the final poem in the sequence "Tales of the Islands" – "I watched till the plane / Turned to the final north", "until all that I love / Folded in cloud" (*Green Night*, 30). The epigraph that had appeared with this poem in its first published version (*Bim*, no. 26, January–June 1958) was "the lake isle", alluding to W.B. Yeats's "The Lake Isle of Innisfree". Significantly, this was replaced in the subsequent version by a phrase from a St Lucian folksong, "*adieu foulard*". This poem marks the definitive beginning of Walcott's poetic record of journey and homecoming.

TWO

The UCWI was still in its infancy, having started teaching, in medicine, only two years earlier (in 1948). The campus was located on the former Mona estate, which had flourished in the days of plantation slavery. It had subsequently been the site of Gibraltar Camp, which had housed evacuees from Gibraltar and Malta during the Second World War. The college was at first housed in the barrack-like buildings of the camp, and the first student hall of residence, where Walcott lived for most of his time at Mona, was named Gibraltar Hall.

The UCWI was founded in affiliation with the University of London, so the degrees offered were degrees of the University of London. Walcott enrolled for the bachelor of arts degree in English, French and Latin. The syllabus in English amounted to a history of the literature of England. Walcott wrote essays on *Sir Gawain and the Green Night*, *Piers Plowman*, Christopher Marlowe, John Webster, Shakespeare, John Donne, George Herbert, Samuel Taylor Coleridge, John Keats and Emily Brontë. In other words, the grounding that he had had at school was being continued. The three lecturers in the English department were white expatriates, and the head of department, Professor A.K. Croston, was a graduate of Cambridge who had studied under the acclaimed F.R. Leavis. One of Walcott's tutors in French, William Mailer, a Scotsman, was impressed by his wide reading, and remembered that he quoted from Dante in a French examination.

Half a century later, as keynote speaker at a "Gathering of Graduates" at Mona, Walcott said: "[F]or most of my sentence here, I despised the place, its jaded, predictable curriculum, for not being the University of the West Indies, as I watched Englishmen guide the direction in which I should go. The format was too familiar."[3] Walcott's poem "Gib Hall Revisited" (*The Gulf*) had prefigured by some twenty-five years this aspect of his "Gathering of Graduates" address. It links the displaced people of Gibraltar Camp, including the Jews, to the British colonial context and the informing principle of the UCWI in his time.

Still, in happy contrast, by way of his extra-curricular activities, the Mona campus also gave Walcott some pleasurable, productive and profitable years, years that strengthened his sense of West Indianness. The range of these activities involved friendships, pursuing his writing, spearheading student activity in creative writing, theatre and painting.

The idea of the West Indies as a place in its own vibrant right was nowhere more alive than among that small but growing group of bright, future-making young people from across the region, living and striving together. As it happened,

CHAPTER TWO

these were the years when the idea of a political federation of the West Indies was gaining ground, and the student body at Mona was one of the idea's most elatedly anticipatory constituencies. After all, the UCWI was itself a federal institution. The West Indies Federation was established in 1958, but by 1962 it fell apart. In "A Map of the Antilles" (*In a Green Night*), written while the federation was in existence, Walcott voices his sense of the tensions involved in the federal idea, between the attraction of the union of states and the attachment to one's native island/territory. "The Lost Federation" (*Sea Grapes*), written after the collapse of the federation, is a sarcastic "cussing out" of West Indian politicians and their betrayal of the people in respect of the federal episode and the drive for "independence".

Walcott was to remember fondly his circle of friends from the Mona days, their beer-drinking nights at the students' union, even the name of the bartender, and the live music of the student band, the Varsity Sextet. He recalls "the false comedy of [the students] mocking one another's origins", and how he "loved to hear" a Barbadian friend, "Sleepy" Smith, "recite Homer in a Bajan accent".[4]

In his Mona days, Walcott also made two close, enduring, non-student friendships that were germane to his role in the development of West Indian literature. These were with the Jamaican poet, critic and educator John Figueroa, and the Jamaican novelist John Hearne. Both, and the part they played in Walcott's knowledge of Jamaican landscape, are memorialized in canto 18, part 1, of *Tiepolo's Hound* (2000). Poem 41 of *White Egrets* (2010) is "In memoriam, John Hearne".

Walcott's *The Castaway* (1965) and *The Gulf* (1970) are dedicated to Hearne, and in the latter "Nearing Forty" is dedicated to Figueroa. Once, Figueroa took Walcott for a drive up into the mountains above Kingston. They looked in at the unoccupied "great house" of a defunct coffee plantation. This experience triggered one of Walcott's best known poems, "Ruins of a Great House".

In an interview with Erika J. Waters, Figueroa spoke of his early, problematic interaction with Walcott, who was one of his students in the diploma in education programme.[5] Having successfully completed his bachelor of arts in 1953, Walcott stayed on at the UCWI to read for the diploma in education. The story is that he had done so reluctantly, not having been able to take up a scholarship to Oxford that was being offered to him. The reason for the delay, according to his mother, was that someone in authority in the St Lucian education system had been too slow to act. Figueroa's explanation is that the UCWI was much too late in releasing the BA results.

Figueroa, who had read some of Walcott's poems on the British Broadcasting Corporation's *Caribbean Voices*, was one of Walcott's lecturers for the diploma. Although Walcott followed the course at best half-heartedly, he was impressed by Figueroa's way of teaching poetry. A legendary Walcott story is that, in a final written examination for Figueroa, in answer to a question relating to Plato and asking examinees to write about the qualities of a good ruler, Walcott wrote one sentence, to the effect that the quality of a good ruler is twelve inches. This story has been recorded by Ralph Thompson, a friend of both Figueroa and Walcott, in his auto-

CHAPTER TWO

biography, *Take My Word for It: A Jamaican Memoir* (2016). What Thompson did not go on to say is that Walcott then left the examination room. He did not get the diploma in education.

The student magazine the *Pelican Annual* (1955, 124) included Walcott in its section "Personalities". Observing that he was "[b]y far the most promising young West Indian poet of our time", the entry on him also observed that "in his perennial blue jeans [he] was a familiar sight" on campus, and that "[m]any remember him more for his quiet wit and quick repartee than for his remarkable genius and versatility". But the genius and versatility were also enrichingly active. He participated in the Scribblers' Group, where students met to read poems they had written and to have them commented on by others in the group. He published his second collection, *Poems*, in 1951. This included poems expressing his unflattering reaction to Jamaican society, including the high-profiling of the tourist industry. The collection, heavily influenced by W.H. Auden, was the work of a poet still searching for his own voice. The only one of the poems that he included in any subsequent collection is "Margaret Verlieu Dies", under the title of the earlier version, "A Country Club Romance", which had appeared in *25 Poems*.

Shortly after he arrived at Mona, Walcott and a few other students, including Stanley ("Bill") Brooks, Harold ("Harry") Drayton and Charlie Pilgrim, started the first student magazine, the *Barb*, a mimeographed production, of which Walcott was the first editor, as well as an illustrator. After two numbers, the magazine's name was changed to the *Pelican* (no. 1, January 1951). Walcott was a leader in the Art Society, and could be observed on campus at work before his easel. Harry Drayton recalled that, one Christmas at Mona, he exchanged two cigarettes with Derek for a painting of a head of Christ.[6] The painter-poet was a steady smoker in those days. Corinne McLarty, another student friend, has spoken of Derek teaching her and Dahlia Patterson to smoke.[7]

It was in theatre that Walcott's genius was most visible: in writing, producing and directing, set design and backdrop painting. He was a leading light in the Dramatic Society, which had been started in 1948 by a group of students led by Owen Minott and Joan Swaby. In its first issue (14 January 1951), the *Pelican* announced that the first production of the society, a Shakespeare play, was to be staged in April 1951, produced by Robert LePage, lecturer in English, Derek Walcott and Joan Swaby. This production was soon put in abeyance, with Sophocles's *Oedipus Rex*, directed by Walcott, replacing it. In 1952, the Dramatic Society presented Walcott's *Harry Dernier*, with the author directing. Then, early in 1954, the production of *Henri Christophe* was a great success. Walcott not only produced and directed, but also designed the set and painted the backdrop mural.

Walcott left the Mona campus in 1954, with a bachelor of arts degree, which he had successfully completed in 1953. However, during the later 1950s his playwriting gift was kept actively alive in the minds of Kingston's theatre-goers and at the UCWI. His one-act play *The Sea at Dauphin* was staged in 1956 on the Mona campus by the University Players, directed by Slade Hopkinson. It had been first staged in Port of Spain in August 1954 by the New Company and the Whitehall Players, directed by Errol Hill. Hill was influential in having the play published by the UCWI's Department of Extra-Mural Studies, as the fourth in its Caribbean Plays series, 1954. The publication is dedicated to Hill. In 1956, Walcott directed his *The Wine of the Country* (never published), produced by Slade Hopkinson, at the Dramatic Theatre, UCWI, Mona. Then, in 1957, Hill directed the premiere of Walcott's *Ione* at the Ward Theatre in Kingston. The play was produced by the Federal Theatre, which Hill had founded, and which was yet another expression of the enthusiastic anticipation, in some circles, of a West Indian federation. In the same year, *Ione*, directed by Walcott himself, was also presented in Trinidad by the Company of Players at the Community Education Extension Workshop in Port of Spain. In 1959 his one-act *Malcauchon* was performed by the West Indian Players of the UCWI at the Dramatic Theatre on the Mona campus. It had been first performed earlier that year, along with another one-act play, *Jourmard*, by the St Lucia Arts Guild in Castries, and under the direction of Roderick Walcott, himself a gifted playwright. These productions were then taken, in the same year, to the Queen's Hall, Port of Spain.

These four plays – *The Sea at Dauphin*, *Malcauchon*, *Ione* and *Jourmard* – all deal with St Lucian subject-matter, mainly with the lot of the common people, "[t]he black, the despairing, the poor", to use his phrase from the poem "Return to D'Ennery, Rain" (*Green Night*, 33). Walcott uses the language of the people, giving them "serious" dramatic voice. In the process, he also blends local folk-performance features with influences from non-West Indian drama. For instance, in *Dauphin*, which adverts to J.M. Synge's *Riders to the Sea*, the Chorus of Dauphin Women naturalized the chorus of Classical Greek tragedy. *Malcauchon; or The Six in the Rain* works to acknowledge the humanity of the socially outcast woodcutter, who internalizes the society's configuration of him as "brute" and "tiger". The play draws, like *Ti-Jean*, on Akira Kurosawa's film *Rashomon*, and on the work of the artist Hokusai. *Ione* attempts to make a tragic family feud between clans in the hill country into a West Indian equivalent of Classical Greek tragedy, a sort of tragedy-of-the-house-of-Atreus. The attempt overreaches itself. The characters and their native speech do not quite match the grand manner of the style of speech that is thrust on them. In *Jourmard, or A Comedy till the Last Minute*, Walcott ventured into satirical comedy. It depicts clever bums in the streets of Castries, begging for money to buy themselves drinks. Ironically, it is Easter Sunday morning and the people being approached for money are on their way to mass. The style and tone of the play recall something of Bertolt Brecht and of the German caricaturist George Grosz.

The actor perhaps most identified, with acclaim, with productions of Walcott plays in Jamaica in the 1950s was Archie Hudson-Phillips, a Trinidadian medical student. He played in *Henri Christophe*, *Wine of the Country*, *Ione* and *The Sea at Dauphin*, winning the Jamaica Adult Drama Festival prize for best actor for his portrayal of Afa in the last-named.

The Mona campus also gave Walcott a wife. He became romantically attached to Faye Moyston, Jamaican, secretary to Philip (later Sir Philip) Sherlock, then director of the college's Department of Extra-Mural Studies. Sherlock, himself a poet and a contributor to the emergence of a distinctive West Indian poetry, was very much aware of the significance of Walcott's presence in the college, and welcomed him. He recalled that Walcott would come to his office at lunch time and borrow the typewriter to type poems for Faye. "[N]ow and again she would get cross at his coming so often and tear one or two and throw them in the wastepaper basket. I wish I had retrieved them."[8] Faye and Derek were married on 25 August 1954 at La Clery Chapel in St Lucia. The marriage produced a son, Peter.

After teaching stints at the Grenada Boys' Secondary School and at his alma mater, St Mary's College, Walcott returned to Jamaica to teach at another high school for boys, Jamaica College. He also began to work as a feature writer for the Jamaican weekly newspaper *Public Opinion*, writing mostly on literature and drama. This arrangement was integral to Walcott's contribution to the bourgeoning of West Indian literature. *Public Opinion*, established in 1937, was the newspaper of the People's National Party, which, under its founding leader Norman Manley, was in the forefront of the Jamaican anti-colonial push to self-government. The paper was also distinctive in its recognition of the importance of the arts and culture to sociopolitical development.

At the time of his association with *Public Opinion*, Walcott lived on Wellington Drive, not far from Jamaica College and the Mona campus of the UCWI. Barbara Gloudon has written: "To be admitted to the inner circle of his Sunday night sessions in his flat at Wellington [Drive] you had to be quick with wit, knowledgeable in the arts and have a skin thicker than a crocodile's. Derek's tongue was razor sharp and many a Sunday night we watched people retreat from the session . . . chopped up because of their lack of knowledge and faltering sense of humour."[9]

By the later 1950s, the dream of a West Indian federation was becoming a reality, and this development was to enhance Walcott's region-wide traction as poet-playwright. When it was decided that the federal parliament of the West Indies was to be inaugurated in Port of Spain early in 1958, the UCWI's Department of Extra-Mural Studies, at the behest of its director, Philip Sherlock, commissioned Walcott to write a pageant to celebrate the opening of the parliament. The result was *Drums and Colours*. This work evokes the historical context out of which the federation emerged, and in that way hailed the idea of the federation. The pageant develops in terms of the stories of "four heroes" (*Haitian Trilogy*, 123): Christopher Columbus and Sir Walter Raleigh, representing the imperialist/colonizer, and Toussaint L'Ouverture and George William Gordon, representing the anti-colonialist liberator. The action is framed in a carnival performance mode, particularly appropriate since the pageant was to be presented in Trinidad. It opened in the Royal Botanical Gardens, Port of Spain, in April 1958, directed by Noel Vaz and Dagmar Butt, and with a cast of actors drawn from across the West Indies.

The commission to write *Drums and Colours* involved a grant from the Rockefeller Foundation, enabling Walcott, along with Vaz and Errol Hill, to travel to Stratford, Ontario, to seek to persuade Tyrone Guthrie, the famous director/producer, to direct *Drums and Colours*. Vaz and Hill were both drama tutors in the UCWI's Department of Extra-Mural Studies, and highly regarded theatre directors in the West Indies. Guthrie declined.

On that trip to Stratford, Walcott had a five-day stopover in New York City, his first time there. He felt terrified by the city and hardly left his hotel room, but during that time, in a surge of longing for St Lucia, he wrote *Ti-Jean and His Brothers*. This surprised him, since he would normally take a long time, sometimes years, to complete a play. *Ti-Jean* was to prove one of his finest and most popular plays.

The success of *Drums and Colours* was no doubt a factor in Walcott's being awarded a Rockefeller Foundation fellowship to study directing under José Quintero at the Circle in the Square Theatre, New York City, between October 1958 and June 1959. Walcott would also go to the Phoenix Theatre to sit in on rehearsals being conducted by Norris Houghton.

THREE

Buoyed by the New York experience, Walcott returned to Trinidad in August 1959 with the intention of developing repertory theatre there. He was to live in Trinidad for nearly two decades, and it became his second home-island. During this period, he made a groundbreaking contribution to the development of West Indian theatre, his poetry gained increasing international acclaim, and he made a too-little-known contribution to the arts and culture of the West Indies by way of journalism.

On arriving in Trinidad, Walcott stayed for a short time with Bruce Procope, a barrister, who had been chairman of the committee overseeing the production of *Drums and Colours*. He then found accommodation in a house on Bengal Street that was shared by two friends: Veronica Jenkin, an English schoolteacher, and Irma "Billie" Pilgrim, a Guyanese librarian. He had been referred to Pilgrim by his friend, the novelist John Hearne. Jenkin and Pilgrim became his friends. The former became a member of Walcott's Little Carib Theatre Workshop, serving both as actor and director. Pilgrim later married Laurence "Laurie" Goldstraw, an Englishman who was to act in some of Walcott's plays. In 1984, she published the definitive *Derek Walcott: An Annotated Bibliography of His Works*. Walcott's poem "Oddjob, a Bull Terrier" (*Sea Grapes*, 1976) was inspired by the death of the Goldstraws' dog, after which the poem is titled.

The house in Bengal Street was a social meeting-place for middle-class aficionados of the arts, a setting just right for the Walcott who had "held court" at Wellington Drive in Kingston. Billie Pilgrim recalls that these were Walcott's drinking days, and that he would have temporary "bust-ups" with friends, being sometimes rude, even insulting. Once he slammed his fist in anger through a glass door at a get-together at a friend's house. She mentioned this in response to my telling her that I had run into Derek in the departure lounge at Seawell (now Grantley Adams) Airport in Barbados. Noticing that his right hand was bandaged, I asked him what had happened. He replied, with a somewhat nuanced look, that he had pushed his hand through a door.

Also involved in the Little Carib Theatre Workshop, behind the scenes, was Margaret Ruth Maillard, a Trinidadian almoner and social worker. A dancer and painter, she was active in the artistic life of Port of Spain. She had been a member of the sound crew for *Drums and Colours*. In the very first show by the Theatre Workshop, in December 1959, she was in charge of properties and front of house. By this time she and Walcott had developed a romantic relationship. (His first marriage had ended in divorce in 1959.) They were married in 1962 and lived at 165 Duke of Edinburgh Avenue, Petit

Valley, in the outskirts of Port of Spain. With their shared interests in the arts, their love was enhanced by vibrant friendship, which they maintained even after divorce. The marriage lasted over fifteen years. Walcott's *Selected Poems* (1974), *Sea Grapes* (1976) and *The Star-Apple Kingdom* (1979) are all dedicated to Margaret. Their marriage was blessed by the birth of two daughters: Elizabeth ("Lizzie") in 1964, and Anna in 1968. Derek's son, Peter, from his first marriage, also lived at Duke of Edinburgh Avenue for quite a few years. Derek's *Midsummer* (1984) is "for Elizabeth and Anna".

Shortly after his return to Trinidad, Walcott, with the help of Beryl McBurnie, celebrated dancer, dance teacher and history-making promoter of the performing arts, started a theatre workshop at her Little Carib Theatre in Woodbrook, Port of Spain. The workshop sessions were held on Friday evenings. However, after a falling-out between Walcott and McBurnie, the Little Carib Theatre Workshop became the Basement Theatre Workshop, when it moved to the basement of the Bretton Hall Hotel on Victoria Avenue. Subsequently, when the Theatre Workshop began staging plays, the Little Carib was a venue.

Soon enough, there was a rift between Walcott and the owner of the Bretton Hall, and the workshop, as the Trinidad Theatre Workshop, went on a restless sequence of relocations, to the pavilion at the zoo in the Royal Botanical Gardens, the Catholic Centre in Coblentz, and the Old Fire Station in downtown Port of Spain. This inability to find a satisfactory, settled theatre space was no doubt the personal frustration that fuelled Walcott's sustained cry for a "proper" theatre

CHAPTER THREE

space in Port of Spain. The facilities at the various locations for the workshop were generally inadequate and challenging. For instance, not only was the basement space small and dark, but the air-conditioning unit was very noisy. A cost factor contributed to some of the inconvenience. At the Little Carib there was no seating for the actors during the long hours of rehearsal; chairs had to be hired for performances.

In an article in the *Sunday Guardian* (15 May 1996, 9) about Walcott's typical working day with the Basement Theatre, Carl Jacobs begins by telling of going to interview Walcott at home. He writes that "[a]t 6.30 p.m. Derek Walcott was still in his pyjamas. He had been working in them all day, re-writing three full-length plays." I had a similar experience in the mid-1970s, when I went to Duke of Edinburgh Avenue at mid-morning to interview Walcott in connection with *Another Life*. He was lying in bed in his pyjamas, writing and sketching. I sat beside the bed and interviewed him for about two hours. I was impressed by his ability to give me his attention and to compose at the same time. He invited me to have lunch with him. Some time after lunch, we went our separate ways, he to a meeting of the Trinidad Theatre Workshop. According to Jacobs (ibid.), after dinner Walcott watched *The Flintstones* on television, while "browsing through . . . a copy of *The Castaway*; then he went to the Basement Theatre to hear some young poets reading their work". Walcott was as avid a fan of television series as he was of movies.

Laurence Goldstraw has said that Walcott "made virtually all the [workshop] decisions himself". He was "very thorough and painstaking, and most of the time extremely patient", but would now and then explode.[10] He could not abide the actors making any changes to his lines. One frustration that they had to experience when they were rehearsing a play written by Walcott was that they would memorize a scene and come prepared to perform it, only to find that Derek had rewritten it. He would also often make them work intensively on a particular small section of a play and ignore the rest of it.

Among Goldstraw's roles were Major Jack Willoughby in *Franklin* and Dr Theodore Holley in *The Charlatan*, in the 1973 productions, the former at the Bishop Anstey High School auditorium, the latter at the Town Hall. The action of *The Charlatan*, a "carnival comedy" with music, takes place on the eve of carnival. This version of the play develops, in respect of its carnival/calypso features, the version produced in 1962. *The Charlatan* was to be further revised for presentation at the Mark Taper Forum, Los Angeles, in 1974, with music by Galt MacDermot, and under the direction of Mel Shapiro. It was presented at the Little Carib Theatre in January 1976. Walcott directly speaks to the carnival factor of the play in the article "Theatre and the Tents in Trinidad" (*Tapia*, 9 January 1976). This article is also more widely instructive in terms of the carnival/calypso features of his plays. Also germane in this regard is his essay "Theatre without Walls", in *Stagebill* (16, no. 3 [November 1988]).

There is a one-act mimeograph version of *Franklin*, apparently the first, in the Mona campus library of the University of the West Indies. It seems reasonable to assume that this was written while Walcott was a student at Mona.

CHAPTER THREE

In 1968, a revised version won first prize in the Barbados Arts Council's competition for three-act plays. Although *Franklin* deals, like Walcott's other plays about the West Indies, with the colonial legacy of the region and the West Indian effort to come to terms with it, a distinguishing feature in this case is that the central figure is the white man, the colonizer, at the end of empire. This figure, Captain Luther Franklin, is presented with critical understanding.

When Walcott started the workshop, he was in no hurry to do productions. For a good little while the focus was on improvising, interacting, feeling the way forward. The first full-scale production (of entire plays) took place in May 1962. One week before it opened, he wrote a letter of invitation to people who he thought would be interested. Before that production, there had been, in December 1959, "Showcase I", an evening of six scenes from four playwrights, together with a dramatization of Samuel Selvon's short story "Basement Lullaby".

Walcott's vision was of a West Indian theatre which, in the representation of West Indianness, engaged with world theatre. He hoped for actors who would speak Shakespeare without affectation, and West Indian dialects poetically, respectfully, beyond just raw humour. His vision is indicated by the plays done over the years. For example, the first season of full plays, in May 1962, offered Samuel Beckett's *Krapp's Last Tape* and *The Caged* by Jamaican Dennis Scott. In December 1962, the Little Carib Theatre Workshop staged Ionesco's *The Lesson* and Walcott's *Malcauchon*. The 1966 season, at/as the Basement Theatre, brought together Jean

Genet's *The Blacks*, Wole Soyinka's *The Road* and Tobagonian Eric Roach's *Belle Fanto*. In 1966, there were programmes of readings: poetry by Roach, Walcott and the Canadian Lionel Kearns; prose fiction by John Hearne and George Lamming.

There was not much West Indian drama to speak of at that time. The most memorable non-Walcott West Indian play presented by the workshop was Errol John's *Moon on a Rainbow Shawl*, staged in its entirety in 1967. The workshop also did, in 1973, *Odale's Choice*, and in 1969 *Stepchild, Stepchild*, by the Barbadians Edward [Kamau] Brathwaite and Oliver Jackman respectively. Walcott no doubt wrote some of his plays with the Theatre Workshop and particular actors in mind. The workshop came to be famously associated with certain Walcott plays, most notably *Dream on Monkey Mountain*, *Ti-Jean and His Brothers* and *The Joker of Seville*. There were also *The Sea at Dauphin*, *Malcauchon*, *The Charlatan*, *O Babylon!*, *Jourmard* and *In a Fine Castle*. *The Joker* premiered at the Little Carib Theatre on 28 November 1974, and *O Babylon!* on 19 March 1976. These productions were all directed by the playwright.

In his plays associated most memorably with his Theatre Workshop period, Walcott not only foregrounded West Indian subject-matter in a serious, thought-provoking way, he also creatively mined West Indian humour and gave literary voice to the West Indian folk. *Ti-Jean* and *Dream* are West Indian classics. The former, as Walcott said, in an article titled "Derek's 'Most West Indian Play'" (*Sunday Guardian Magazine*, 21 June 1970), grew out of a folktale told by a schoolmate, about a peasant woman and her three sons responding to a

CHAPTER THREE

challenge from the Devil. It was first performed at the Little Carib Theatre in 1958, with Errol Jones as Devil, before the Theatre Workshop had come into being. It was revived in June 1970 by the Trinidad Theatre Workshop. Coming so soon after *Drums and Colours*, *Ti-Jean* heightened Walcott's presence in Trinidad as playwright.

Walcott's dramatization of the fable is enhanced by his incorporation of two examples of folk performance. He uses an oral storytelling framework by way of a narrator-chorus of animals. Also, threading through the play and heightening the drama of the sons' confrontation with the Devil, is a traditional St Lucian form of theatre of the streets, the Christmas masquerade of the Devil, which he described, also in the *Sunday Guardian Magazine* (25 December 1966), in a piece titled "The White Devil: A Story of Christmas". So *Ti-Jean* is at once both distinctively local/St Lucian and universal, the struggle between Good and Evil. In "Derek's 'Most West Indian Play'", the playwright recognizes not only the Africa-derived storytelling tradition, but also, in the form and style, suggestions of Federico García Lorca, Bertolt Brecht and Japanese Noh theatre. Then again, inasmuch as the Devil is the White Planter, this universal fable grows out of and speaks to West Indian colonial history and the struggle of the oppressed for liberation.

The Theatre Workshop's first production of *Dream*, directed by Walcott, was at Queen's Hall, Port of Spain, in January 1968. It had been previously staged, at the Central Library Theatre, Toronto, in August 1967. It tells how Makak (monkey), a poor, uneducated, alcoholic charcoal burner from the deep country, comes to find his personhood. This process involves his rejection of his fealty to the White Goddess of his dream-vision, as well as of the compensatory dream of a romanticized Africa in which he is a king. The play was performed in Port of Spain by the Theatre Workshop at a time when the Black Power movement, at its height in the United States, was taking hold in Trinidad and Tobago. The movement became a leading factor in an attempted overthrow of the government of the republic in February 1970.

This attempt was driven by a loose coalition of radical students at the St Augustine campus of the University of the West Indies, leaders of the trade union movement, and disaffected officers of the army. There was some violence and a few deaths, and a state of emergency was declared. Among the public there were sharp differences of reaction to this development. Walcott was not exactly enthusiastic about the uprising, as one can detect in his important, much-cited essay "What the Twilight Says: An Overture", written in February 1970; or in his answer to Edward Hirsch's question, in 1977, about the relationship of the West Indian writer to Africa: "I was writing against the African influence during a period when the political nostalgia [for Africa] seemed to be a deceit."[11] In an interview with Walcott in 1973, Raoul Pantin asked him to explain the reason for his apparent disaffection with the attempted revolution. Walcott replied: "The thing fell apart for me when it took the direction of being not only a black revolution but of being blacker than thou."[12]

At a conference of the Association for Commonwealth Literature and Language Studies held at the Mona campus of

CHAPTER THREE

the University of the West Indies in January 1970, there was a mischievous rumour that Walcott, who had been invited, had chosen not to attend because he knew he would not be welcome, being too Eurocentric and not sufficiently black in his poetics. Amusingly, and ironically, the front cover of the first edition (1993) of Hamner's *Critical Perspectives on Derek Walcott* carries a 1975 photograph of a seemingly politically correct Walcott, wearing an Afro hairstyle and a colourful dashiki.

Walcott's play *In a Fine Castle*, a re-working of *Wine of the Country*, was first produced by the Creative Arts Centre, University of the West Indies, Mona, Jamaica, in October 1970. It speaks indirectly to the attempted revolution. This production, directed by Walcott, marked the beginning of a fertile collaboration between him and Richard Montgomery and Sally Thompson (soon to be Mrs Montgomery), set designer and costume designer respectively. Walcott had come to the Mona campus a few months earlier, at the invitation of the university, to be visiting playwright/director at the centre. *In a Fine Castle* was staged by the Trinidad Theatre Workshop in December 1971 at Queen's Hall, Port of Spain. Walcott substantially reworked the play as *The Last Carnival*, which was first staged in 1982, but more of this in the next chapter.

The Joker of Seville, Walcott's adaptation of Tirso de Molina's *El burlador de Sevilla*, was first performed at the Little Carib theatre in November–December 1974, to mark the fifteenth anniversary of the Trinidad Theatre Workshop. The fact that it was commissioned by the Royal Shakespeare Company is an indication of how far Walcott's reputation had reached by then. The suggestion that Walcott do the adaptation had been made to the Royal Shakespeare Company by their literary advisor, Ronald Bryden, to whom *The Joker* is dedicated. Although it was never staged by the Royal Shakespeare Company, *The Joker* became the workshop's most resounding success in Trinidad. Sensing a populist grounding and reach in de Molina's play, Walcott reimagined it happily into a Trinidadian–West Indian mode, in the humour, the "playing mas'" and, what is perhaps the most engaging aspect, the music: Walcott's variety of catchy lyrics made all the more memorable by the music of Galt MacDermot, composer for the Broadway hit musical *Hair*. There was to be subsequent collaboration between Walcott and MacDermot, but the impact of *The Joker* was never equalled.

The success of *Joker* no doubt added impetus to Walcott's move to his next play, another musical, also to draw on Galt MacDermot, and with one eye seemingly set on Broadway. This was *O Babylon!*, about a Rastafarian community in Kingston at the time of the Emperor Haile Selassie's visit to Jamaica. The play was first staged by the Trinidad Theatre Workshop in March 1976, in association with Michael Butler, under Walcott's direction and with music by MacDermot, at the Little Carib Theatre. Butler, the producer of *Hair*, had suggested to Walcott and MacDermot that they write a musical that might "make" Broadway.

In contrast to the carnivalesque fun of *Joker*, *O Babylon!* dramatizes class injustice in the postcolonial West Indies. The Rastafarian squatters on "captured" land are evicted by a collusion between the sociopolitical establishment and "big business". The plot moves between anticipating the disastrous effects of the eviction and the jubilation at the impending arrival of Haile Selassie, whom the Rastafarians regard as God. The play had mixed reviews and was not nearly the success of *Joker*. Walcott does not quite catch the energy and inventiveness of Rastafarian speech, "dread talk", and the Rastafarians appear as little more than misguided, sentimental idealists. What is more, MacDermot's music does not catch reggae nearly as well as he had reproduced calypso.

To think of the contribution of the Trinidad Theatre Workshop to West Indian drama is to think inevitably of the excellence of many of the actors. They made the workshop as much as the workshop made them: Errol Jones, Albert LaVeau, Stanley Marshall, Wilbert Holder, Hamilton Parris, Nigel Scott, Ermine Wright and others. Some of them are inseparably identified with roles they played, for example: Jones with Makak, LaVeau with Planter/Devil, Marshall with Moustique, Wright with Mother (*Ti-Jean*), Scott with Don Juan. They have all spoken with admiration and gratitude for Walcott's influence on their careers in theatre. Jones, a founding member of the workshop, had, before meeting Walcott, acted in *Drums and Colours*, as well as in *Henri Christophe* and *The Sea at Dauphin* (in which he played the lead role), both directed by Errol Hill. There was also Slade Hopkinson, but he had established himself as a brilliant actor, and had worked with Walcott, before the Trinidad Theatre Workshop years.

The West Indian reach of the workshop was extended when they began to make tours in the region. In October 1968, they toured Grenada, St Lucia, Barbados, Antigua and St Vincent, in that order. In July 1969, they took *Ti-Jean and His Brothers* to Grenada, St Lucia and Barbados. Then came a major advance, three highly successful tours to Jamaica: with *Dream* and *Ti-Jean* in 1971, *Franklin* and *The Charlatan* in 1973, and *The Joker* in 1975. These tours were handsomely sponsored by Pan-Jamaican Investment Trust Limited, through the mediation of their managing director Ralph Thompson, himself a poet and Walcott's friend. Most fittingly, Walcott's book of two plays, *The Joker of Seville & O Babylon!*, is dedicated to Thompson and his wife, Doreen.

The impact of Walcott's theatrical gift had reached even farther afield, when, in 1971, *Dream on Monkey Mountain*, performed Off-Broadway by the Negro Ensemble Company, won an Obie Award for Best Foreign Play. In July 1972, *Ti-Jean and His Brothers*, with music by Andre Tanker, was produced by Joseph Papp at the Delacorte Theater in Central Park. The cast was largely American, but Albert Laveau was outstanding as Devil/Planter/Papa Bois.

※

Settling in Trinidad in 1959, with his sights set on starting a theatre workshop, Walcott needed some source of income. He soon began to work as a feature writer for the *Trinidad Guardian* and was extremely productive over the next fifteen years or so, focusing mainly on literature, the arts (including performing arts), culture and society. Raoul Pantin,

CHAPTER THREE

Trinidadian journalist, playwright and poet, first met Walcott when he joined the *Guardian* as a junior reporter in 1965. He found Walcott "a vague and distant newsroom presence, an aloof man who wrote long esoteric articles".[13] "Long" and "esoteric" to describe some of Walcott's articles may represent one view of what may otherwise be seen as the relatively high quality of those articles.

Gordon Collier has performed an invaluable service for Walcott scholars by collecting, editing and publishing these journalistic pieces in two volumes, under the title *The Journeyman Years: Occasional Prose 1957–1974* (2013). The volumes also include Walcott's pieces in *Public Opinion* (Jamaica), *Caribbean Contact* (Trinidad), the *Gleaner* (Jamaica), *Tapia* (later *Trinidad and Tobago Review*), and the *Voice of St Lucia*. These largely unknown journalistic pieces by Walcott enhance understanding not only of his own ideas and creative imagination, but also of West Indian literature and drama at a crucial stage of their development and of West Indian literary criticism, then still in its infancy.

A few illustrations will suffice. Prose fiction was in the forefront of the bourgeoning of a West Indian literature, and Walcott's reviewing covers most of the novelists who established themselves during the period in question, notably Michael Anthony, Austin Clarke, Wilson Harris, John Hearne, Edgar Mittelholzer, V.S. Naipaul and Samuel Selvon. Those interested in following the story of Walcott's conflicted response to Naipaul must read these Walcott pieces on Naipaul, which include a highly complimentary, astute review of *A House for Mr Biswas*. There is even an interview with

Naipaul, the existence of which may come as a surprise to many. There is also a searching essay on the West Indian short story. The poets are not neglected. They include Kamau (L. Edward) Brathwaite and John Figueroa. Of more than historic significance is Walcott's recurrent attention to Frank Collymore's little magazine *Bim*. Walcott's critical appreciation is not confined to anglophone Caribbean literature. He gives an appreciable amount of attention to Aimé Césaire, T.S. Eliot and Ernest Hemingway, Eliot and Hemingway being both very much in the forefront of literary-minded West Indians of Walcott's generation. His "On the Necessity of Negritude" (*Trinidad Guardian*, 28 September 1964), was written to celebrate president of Senegal Leopold Senghor on the occasion of his state visit to Trinidad and Tobago.

A fortuitous spin-off from the newspaper work was the friendship between Walcott and Donald "Jackie" Hinkson, who was to become one of Trinidad and Tobago's most acclaimed artists. Walcott's first mention of Hinkson was in a review of an exhibition by five young painters, which appeared in the *Trinidad Guardian* on 10 August 1961, one month before Hinkson's nineteenth birthday. Other reviews were to follow in the early 1960s. Walcott found Hinkson's work arresting and of much promise. They eventually became friends and for decades Walcott regularly attended Hinkson's New Year's Eve party. In October/November 1998, Colbert Nepaulsingh, professor of comparative literature at the State University of New York at Albany, arranged a joint exhibition at the University Art Museum by the two friends, under the caption *Island Light: Watercolours and Oil Paintings by Derek*

CHAPTER THREE

Walcott and Donald Hinkson. Nepaulsingh was to be co-editor of a fully annotated edition of *Another Life* in 2004.

The 1960s also saw a decisive escalation in Walcott's standing as poet. In 1962, while his Theatre Workshop was beginning to gather momentum, his first collection of poems to be published outside the Caribbean appeared, when Jonathan Cape of London published *In a Green Night: Poems 1948–1960*. In 1960, he had begun to have poems published in Alan Ross's *London Magazine*. One of these, "A Sea-Chantey", won the 1961 Guinness Award for Poetry. Through Ross, Walcott had come to the attention of Tom Maschler of Cape. On being sent a copy of *In a Green Night*, Robert Graves wrote: "Walcott handles English with a closer understanding of its inner magic than most (if not any) of his English-born contemporaries." This was to be quoted on the jacket of Walcott's next two books of poetry, as well as frequently after that by people writing on Walcott.

Walcott's international publication record, for books of poetry, was to widen when his *Selected Poems* (dedicated to Margaret) was published by New York's Farrar, Straus and Company in 1964. Cape had sent Robert Giroux of Farrar, Straus a copy of *In a Green Night*, and Giroux had asked Robert Lowell for a report on it. Lowell commended it. Walcott had met Lowell before this. In 1962, Lowell and his wife Elizabeth Hardwick, on their way to Brazil to visit Elizabeth Bishop, in the course of a lecture tour of South America, stopped off in Trinidad, where Lowell was to do a reading. Lowell had heard of Walcott from Giroux. Walcott, in his capacity as journalist, met Lowell and Hardwick at the airport. The *Trinidad Guardian* carried an article by Walcott captioned "Poet from the Land of the Bean and the Cod: Derek Walcott Meets Robert Lowell" (10 June 1962). After Lowell's death in 1977, Walcott wrote the poem "R.T.S.L." (*The Star-Apple Kingdom*) in memory of him.

Derek and Margaret invited Robert and Elizabeth to spend some time with them at a beach cottage. The holiday together was a happy one, which augured well for the future. Walcott felt especially honoured that Lowell showed him his recently published *Imitations* and asked Walcott's opinion of the poems. Walcott and Lowell ("Cal") became friends but, as Walcott recounts in his moving tribute "On Robert Lowell" (*What the Twilight Says*), the friendship fell on bad times when Lowell insulted Walcott by accusing Walcott of "using" him in his poetry. Years later, there was an emotional reconciliation when Lowell invited Walcott to his apartment, apologized and produced from his jacket pocket a snapshot, which Walcott had long known, of Cal's daughter, Harriet, and Derek's son, Peter, at the beach house in Trinidad.

In the range of topics broached in *In a Green Night*, we see the poet identifying with his landscape and with his people, addressing their difficult history, and his commitment to the poetic vocation in negotiating these themes. We hear him working at his craft under various poetic influences, from T.S. Eliot to Andrew Marvell (in "In a Green Night"), from whom the title of the collection and of the title poem is taken. We hear him moving between a plain, direct style and one in which the poem's meaning works itself indirectly out through a subtlety of metaphorical texture, between a relatively "flat"

CHAPTER THREE

sound and the resonant rhythms to which he was drawn by his early reading.

More than half of the poems in *Selected Poems* were taken from *In a Green Night*. All but two of the remaining sixteen were to reappear in *The Castaway and Other Poems* (Cape, 1965). When he first saw the published book, Walcott told Maschler how pleased he was with it, and made particular mention of the cover. By 1968, he had two new books ready, one provisionally titled "Homecoming", which was to become *The Gulf*, and the other *Another Life*. Maschler was eager for the two books to be published in the autumn of 1968. It was agreed that Maschler would try to negotiate collaboration with Farrar, Straus. As things turned out, Cape published *The Gulf and Other Poems* in 1969. In 1970 Farrar, Straus and Giroux published *The Gulf*. The slight difference in the two titles is significant. The American publication included not only all the poems in the British publication, but also thirteen poems from *The Castaway*, to which Walcott had made small changes.

In *The Castaway* and *The Gulf*, Walcott's concern to get at the plain, unvarnished truth of things is sharpened. He turns a harsher gaze on life, on his sociohistorical environment, on himself. While not abandoning the resonant line or richly metaphorical texture, he now varies these with a relatively plain, "flat" speech. It is, as it were, a movement between "Marlowe's mighty line" and the plain speaking of Edward Thomas, whose poetry, not Walcottian, he greatly admired. Indicatively, *The Gulf* includes "Homage to Edward Thomas". The title poems of the two collections illustrate something of the range of their thematic concerns. "The Castaway" shines its light on the persona as a Robinson Crusoe figure, cut off from the world that produced him, thrown back on himself, challenged to make a new world out of apparent nothing. In "The Gulf", the ominous American racial gulf between peoples reflects all the "othering" that has afflicted human history, as sharply evident in West Indian history.

The 1970s saw the increase of Walcott's poetic productivity, steadily and to acclaim. *Another Life* finally appeared in 1973, after much agonized reworking. A striking addition to twentieth-century attempts at a long narrative poem, it was at once a poem, an autobiography and a novel of sorts, with characters and plot. Its first draft was a prose manuscript, completed in 1966, which had emerged out of his having to write the essay "On Leaving School" for Alan Ross and the *London Magazine*. Telling the story of his St Lucian life up to when he left for Jamaica, it is his *Portrait of the Artist as a Young Man*. The last of the book's four sections, "The Estranging Sea", clarifies what had been lost in his leaving, by describing what he finds on his return. However, the poem ends on an affirmative note, recalling that he and Gregorias, in their commitment to poetry and painting, had been blessed "with Adam's task" of naming their island, of inscribing it in verse and in paint. He was never to abandon that commitment.

The ideas of estrangement, separation and loss in *Another Life*, and the tension between these and the deep identification with one's place and people, are echoed, variously, in *Sea Grapes* and *The Star-Apple Kingdom*. This tension, seen as a legacy of West Indian colonial history, is played out, for example, in "The Schooner *Flight*", one of Walcott's most

CHAPTER THREE

popular poems, a sequence in a modified Trinidadian English Creole, whose protagonist Shabine, "a red nigger who love the sea" (*Star-Apple*, 4), is a mask for the poet. There are other poems, more so in *Sea Grapes*, which speak out against the sociopolitical establishment, the betrayal of the hopes of the people, the corruption of a would-be Eden, poems such as "Preparing for Exile", "Party Night at the Hilton", "The Lost Federation", "Parades, Parades", "New World". These poems obviously owe something to the political upheaval in Trinidad and Tobago in the early 1970s. The title poem of *The Star-Apple Kingdom*, in the mode of the Colombian novelist Gabriel García Márquez, represents favourably the attempt of the then prime minister of Jamaica, Michael Manley, to improve the condition of the people through his policy of democratic socialism.

There are also poems in *Sea Grapes* which reflect on the United States, on Walcott's sense of the landscape and his locating himself in it. These include poems in which he characteristically "enters" landscape and social environment through the work of poets who come out of that landscape and social environment: "Over Colorado" (Walt Whitman), "Spring Street in '58" (Frank O'Hara), "Ohio, Winter" (James Wright). Similarly, there are poems in which, in England, he works through his conflicted relationship to the seat of empire. Perhaps most trenchant, though, with a sort of poignant elation, are the poems which deepen the acknowledgement of the gifts of life and love despite loss and death. Most tellingly, there is the definitive "Sainte Lucie", which takes his "naming" of his island and his identification with it to a poignant height: "moi c'est gens St Lucie. / C'est la moi sorti; / is there that I born".

Sea Grapes and *The Star-Apple Kingdom* also engage, variously, the recurrent, central Walcott theme of creative writers and writing, especially poetry, the hostility it arouses in dictatorial political regimes, and its capacity to evoke "awe, / which has been lost in our time" (*Sea Grapes*, 62). In *Sea Grapes*, we find "Volcano" (Joseph Conrad), "Preparing for Exile" (Osip Mandelstam) and "For Pablo Neruda"; in *The Star-Apple Kingdom* "R.T.S.L." and "Forest of Europe" (Joseph Brodsky).

The later 1970s was an unsettling time for Walcott, ushering in far-reaching change. There was his break with the Trinidad Theatre Workshop in 1976, the breakdown of his marriage with Margaret, and the burgeoning of his love-affair with Norline Metivier, an actress and dancer with the Trinidad Theatre Workshop. She had played the role of Aminta in the 1974 premiere of *The Joker of Seville*. These developments no doubt bore a relationship to his relocation from Trinidad to the United States. He and Metivier got married in Brookline, Massachusetts, in 1982, but within about four years they were separated. Walcott's *Three Plays* (1986) is dedicated to her, as is his *O Babylon!*

In the autumn of 1979, Walcott was writer-in-residence at the College of the Virgin Islands in St Thomas, US Virgin Islands. There he wrote the musical *Marie Laveau*, which premiered at the Little Theatre, College of the Virgin Islands, under his direction. It tells the story of the New Orleans creole voodoo priestess of the play's name. The audience on

CHAPTER THREE

the whole received it favourably, but it was perhaps too obviously an indication of Walcott's aiming at Broadway, too stereotypical in plot and characterization.

His *Remembrance*, commissioned by the Courtyard Players, St Croix, had been staged at the Dorsch Centre, St Croix, US Virgin Islands, in April 1977. It was then presented by Joseph Papp's New York Shakespeare Festival in April 1979. His *Pantomime* had premiered for All Theatre Productions at the Little Carib Theatre in April 1978, under the direction of Albert LaVeau. These are two of Walcott's most satisfying, most popular and most frequently produced plays.

Remembrance is the story-portrait of a retired schoolmaster of a disappearing vintage, one of those who passed on to their students what Walcott, through the voice of his Shabine, called, half-tongue-in-cheek but feelingly, "a sound colonial education" (*Star-Apple*, 4). A nice blend of humour, wonderment and critical respect, the play is Walcott's tribute to such teachers. Appropriately, his mother, Alix, is one of the three people to whom the play is dedicated. The play was also an advance for Walcott in his representation of women, in that the schoolmaster's wife, herself a teacher, is portrayed as a real, flesh-and-blood woman, "warts and all", invested with agency.

Pantomime also deals with the colonial legacy in the Caribbean. In this two-hander comedy, a version of the Empire writing back, he turns on its head the archetypal story of Robinson Crusoe and Man Friday, which had figured in a few of his poems. The published text of the play is dedicated to Wilbert Holder, who played Jackson Phillip (Friday) in the first production.

FOUR

It was a fairly busy time of transition for Walcott, between his being based in Trinidad and his settling in Boston. In the early 1980s, he did short teaching stints at Columbia, Harvard and Yale. In the autumn of 1981, he attended rehearsals of his new play, *Beef, No Chicken*, which opened at the Yale Repertory Theatre in January 1982. It had been first produced by the Trinidad Theatre Workshop at the Little Carib Theatre, Port of Spain, in April 1981. One year later, another new play, *The Isle Is Full of Noises*, had its premiere in Hartford, Connecticut.

His reputation soared with the award of a MacArthur Foundation Fellowship in June 1981, and he accepted the position of visiting professor in the Department of English at Boston University, beginning in January 1982, to teach creative writing. In 1986 his title was normalized to that of professor. He was offered tenure, but declined the offer. His most outstanding contribution to the university was his founding and directing of the Boston Playwrights Theatre. He was to remain at Boston University for twenty-five years. He lived

CHAPTER FOUR

in a condominium at 71 St Mary Street. From there it was a short walk across the bridge and up Commonwealth Avenue to the university. Walcott never drove a motor vehicle.

One important advantage of Walcott's stay at Boston University was that it enabled him to facilitate the higher education of his daughters. They both took degrees from the university. Both have attested to the good parenting which they experienced. In Anna's words, her father was "very devoted, supportive, caring, kind", and "a doting, absolutely besotted grandfather".[14] Walcott's son Peter also lived with him for a time at St Mary Street and studied at a college of architecture.

In his time at Boston, Walcott made his international mark as teacher. Some who were to become outstanding poets and playwrights benefited from his teaching and remember him with admiration and gratitude. Among these are Elizabeth Alexander, Melissa Green, Dan Hunter, Russell Lees, Glyn Maxwell, Ronan Noone and Kate Snodgrass, to name just a few.

To illustrate: Noone, an Irishman, had immigrated to the United States with his heart set on playwriting, but with no concrete plans as to furthering his ambition. Walcott was impressed by the play he submitted with his application to the Boston Playwrights Theatre, and Noone's career was made. When Walcott retired from the Boston Playwrights Theatre, Noone and Melinda Lopez, another of his former students, were appointed to teach his classes. Noone has said that he would not have been where he is today were it not for the guidance and encouragement of Walcott.[15]

When Glyn Maxwell, a young Englishman with a bachelor of arts degree from Oxford, enrolled at Boston University in 1987 to read for a master's in poetry and playwriting, he knew little or nothing about Walcott. When the student-teacher relationship began, they were mutually impressed. A close friendship developed between him and Walcott, and they collaborated in literary appearances. He regularly visited Walcott in St Lucia during Nobel Laureate Week. On the occasion of Walcott's eighty-fourth birthday in 2004, he and Walcott read their poems and conversed for the British Broadcasting Corporation's Radio 4 programme *Derek Walcott: A Fortunate Traveller*, recorded at Walcott's home. He delivered the Derek Walcott Lecture, "To a Breathing Balance: Notes on *The Prodigal*", in 2008, and he edited the well-received collection of *The Poetry of Derek Walcott 1948–2013* (2014).

Kate Snodgrass studied under Walcott in 1987–1988, then stayed on at the Boston Playwrights Theatre to assist him, eventually being appointed artistic director in 2002, and professor of the practice of playwriting in 2012. Playwright and actress, she has won awards as a teacher of playwriting and theatre arts, as well as for her plays. She became a good friend of Walcott's. Like Noone, she visited him regularly in St Lucia during Nobel Laureate Week.

Walcott's teaching style and approach resonated with his students, even if at first somewhat disturbingly. His method was to discommode them at the outset, to pull the rug of complacency from under their feet. He might ask them what made them think they could be poets. He would ask them to recite, or write down from memory, a poem that had impressed them.

CHAPTER FOUR

If, as usually happened, they failed to do so, they felt the sting of his displeasure. He is himself impressive by virtue of his ability to recite a poem by some famous poet, often a poem quite different in character from his own poetry. He stressed to his students the necessity of regarding poetry as the product of hard work and discipline, and not just an expression of self and feeling. This meant, for instance, spending a whole morning agonizing over whether to use the indefinite article, "a", or the definite "the" in a given phrase.

His playwriting students would be jolted to find that when they came to present to him a finished scene, having written and rehearsed it to what seemed like a satisfactory stage, he would, after only a minute or two of the presentation, tell them to stop, and then ask seemingly infuriating questions about it. This eventually opened their eyes to hitherto unseen potential in what they were doing. However, along with these jolting tactics in his teaching method, there was great generosity and encouragement. He would invite some of his playwriting students to sit in on his poetry classes, which many of them did, to their benefit. And discussion would sometimes continue, jovially, in impromptu gatherings in a cafeteria. Just as Walcott never drove a car, so he was never a cook. As Jeremy Taylor writes, "Walcott eats out a lot at nearby restaurants",[16] such as Dunkin Donuts, the Kangaroo Cafe and Chef Chang's. He also liked to relax at the cinema.

A few years after joining the faculty of Boston University, Walcott fortuitously met the person who was to become his life partner. On 19 October 1986, he took part in a reading at the Carnegie Library, Pittsburgh, to celebrate the twentieth anniversary of the International Poetry Forum. In the audience was Sigrid Nama, an art dealer of German-Belgian origin. Her dealership, Antique Prints, specialized in American originals. After the reading, when the poets were signing their books, she went to ask Walcott to sign a book of his that she had bought. They struck up a conversation. He asked if she could take him back to his hotel. She did. The mutual attraction between them grew. As it happened, she had sold her art dealership one week before meeting Walcott, in order to read full-time for a master's degree in art history at the University of Pittsburgh. Vivacious and outspoken, in due course she moved in to live with Walcott at St Mary Street. She first went to St Lucia with him for year-end 1986/1987. Their partnership lasted for thirty years, longer than the combined time of his three marriages. She was lovingly supportive of her *dou-dou* (sweetie-pie) as she called him, using the St Lucian expression.

Walcott's years in the United States were also enriched and made all the more pleasurable by friendships with other famous writers. There was Robert Lowell, of course, as well as Arthur Miller, Mark Strand, August Wilson, Glyn Maxwell and Caryl "Caz" Phillips; but the closest and most famous friendships were with fellow Nobel laureates Seamus Heaney (Irish) and Joseph Brodsky (Russian). Anyone who saw and heard them together was struck by how comfortably and spiritedly they engaged one another. Caryl Phillips has recounted the occasion when he interviewed Walcott in his Brookline apartment. Near the end of the interview, Heaney arrived, whereupon Walcott immediately phoned Brodsky. "They all partook of a loud and lively three-way conversation."[17]

Walcott first met Brodsky at Lowell's funeral in Boston in September 1977. Walcott was seated in a pew with Roger Straus, Susan Sontag and Pat Strachan, when Brodsky, whom he did not know, entered and sat next to him. After the service, they were introduced to each other and the friendship began. In the early 1980s, when Walcott had to go to New York City from Boston for an assignment, he would stay in Brodsky's flat in Greenwich Village. In January 1980, in celebration of Walcott's fiftieth birthday, Brodsky joined Mark Strand and Walcott in an evening of readings of poetry at the Little Carib Theatre in Port of Spain.

Soon enough, Walcott was to celebrate Brodsky in the poem "Forest of Europe", which is not only "For Joseph Brodsky", but about him and the political persecution of poets. Brodsky is a central presence in Walcott's *Midsummer* (1984). The collection opens and closes by directly addressing him. By invoking his friend, Walcott foregrounds the themes of friendship, wandering, exile, the tyranny of totalitarian systems of government and the importance of poetry in dealing with these concerns. Walcott again recalls Brodsky in "4: III" of *The Prodigal* (2004). On 15 February 1988, Brodsky shared the stage with Heaney, Walcott and Wallace Shawn, in "An Evening with Joseph Brodsky", an evening of poetry and drama directed by Andreas Teuber, at the Loeb Drama Center, Brandeis University.

On 28 October 1996, after Brodsky's death in January of

that year, Walcott, along with Susan Sontag, Mark Strand and Tatyana Tolstoya, paid tribute to Brodsky at the Miller Theatre, Columbia University, with readings from, and comments on Brodsky's work. In March 2011, at the American Academy in Rome, Walcott and five other writers, including Strand and Adam Zagajewski, presented "A Tribute to Joseph Brodsky". Brodsky had been a resident at the academy in 1981. The presenters read from their own work as well as Brodsky's, and conversed about Brodsky's life and work.

Walcott memorialized Brodsky in "Italian Eclogues (for Joseph Brodsky)", an elegiac sequence of six poems that appeared in *The Bounty* (1997). The sequence extends the themes which Walcott had identified with Brodsky in *Midsummer*, foregrounding the importance of landscape in Brodsky's poetry, and adverting to Ovid (Publius Ovidius Naso), the prototype of the exiled poet:

> Say you haven't vanished, you're still in Italy.
> Yeah. Very still. God. Still as the turning fields
> of Lombardy, still as the white wastes of that prison
> like pages erased by a regime. Though this landscape heals
> the exile you shared with Naso, poetry is still treason
> because it is truth. Your poplars spin in the sun.
>
> (*Bounty*, 64)

Walcott's collection of essays, *What the Twilight Says* (1998), was dedicated "In Memory J.B".

Walcott first made contact with Seamus Heaney in the late 1970s, after Heaney's complimentary review of *The Star-Apple Kingdom* had appeared in *Parnassus*.[18] Walcott sent him a thank-you note and they met in a New York pub. Another review, this time A. Alvarez's of Heaney's *Field Work* (*New York Review of Books*, 5 March 1980) further boosted the friendship. Walcott was upset by Alvarez's description of Heaney as "a sort of blue-eyed boy". He sent a note to Heaney through his editor at Farrar, Straus and Giroux. "From then on", he told Edward Hirsch, "the friendship developed".[19] They met often when they were both teaching in Boston, Walcott at Boston University and Heaney at Harvard. An attribute that distinguished the rapport between them was their sense of humour, Irish and West Indian, mocking, barbed, self-deflating, off-key.

Heaney was often to visit Walcott in St Lucia during Nobel Laureate Week, sometimes staying at his friend's guest cottage. In Nobel Laureate Week 2005, celebrating Walcott's seventy-fifth birthday, Heaney and Walcott were the main attractions in an evening of readings with a few Caribbean poets: Robert Lee, Kendel Hippolyte, Jane King, Edward Baugh and Ralph Thompson. At the Walcott lecture, "Travelling with Walcott", delivered by Baugh the following evening, question time elicited repeated protestations which implied that Walcott was not "black" enough, not sufficiently representative of "the people", in his poetry. Thompson recalls that, hearing "Baugh [try] to deal diplomatically with the heckling", Heaney "stood up beside Walcott in the front row and quoted Gerard Manley Hopkins that it is love, not ideology, that ultimately defines a poet's greatness".[20]

In that same week, Walcott and Sigrid took a few people to see Dunstan St Omer's altarpiece at the Church of the

Holy Family at Jacmel, overlooking the Roseau Valley, the painting celebrated by Walcott in his poem "For the Altarpiece of the Roseau Valley Church, Saint Lucia" (*Sea Grapes*). The group included Seamus and Marie Heaney, Edward and Sheila Baugh, Ralph Thompson and Gerd Stern. As the guests walked around, admiring the painting, Walcott could be seen leafing through a copy of his *Collected Poems*, which he had brought along. Eventually, finding the poem, he beckoned the guests to be seated. With them facing the altarpiece, and him facing them, one foot up on the pew in front of him, he proceeded to read the poem. It was an unforgettable moment.

Walcott dedicated to Heaney his 1987 collection, *The Arkansas Testament*. Heaney and Brodsky were featured at a conference in the Dublin Millennium Festival at Dun Laoghaire, County Dublin in June 1988. Other participants included Susan Sontag, Chinua Achebe and Luisa Valenzuela. When Heaney received the Nobel Prize in 1995, the trio of Nobel Laureate friends was complete, Brodsky having received his in 1987.

October 2008 saw a disappointing collaboration between Walcott and Heaney: the production of an opera version of Heaney's play *The Burial at Thebes* at London's Globe Theatre, directed by Walcott, with music by the Trinidadian composer Dominique LeGendre. The play, based on Sophocles's *Antigone*, had been first performed to some acclaim in 2004 in Dublin, by the Irish Repertory Theatre, which had commissioned it. However, the operatic version at the Globe found little favour with the critics. They were particularly unimpressed by Le Gendre's music and Walcott's staging and direction. The only aspect that found some favour was Heaney's text.

CHAPTER FOUR

In March 2013, Walcott and Heaney appeared together as keynote presenters at the Association of Writers and Writing Programmes conference in Boston. After reading from their works, the two took part in a discussion moderated by Rosanna Warren. Six months later, Heaney died. Perhaps his most memorable expression of his friendship with Walcott is his poem "Postscript to St Lucia". From faraway Dublin it recalls, with deep yet light-hearted delight, his visits with Walcott in St Lucia.[21] Walcott's portrait of Heaney hangs on the wall of his studio at Cap.

Walcott had not been teaching long in the United States when, in June 1982, the *New York Times* and the *Economist* reported that a charge of sexual harassment had been brought against him by a female student at Harvard. The student, who chose not to be named, claimed that he gave her a C grade for her work in his poetry workshop because she had rejected his advances. Walcott denied the allegation. Harvard investigated the complaint, gave the student a passing grade, and said that it had taken formal action (unspecified) against Walcott. He offered to resign from his substantive post at Boston University, but the university declined to accept his offer. Later in 1982, he was again accused of sexual harassment by a student at Boston.

Then, in 1996, Nicole Niemi, who had been a student in his playwriting class at Boston in autumn 1993, accused him of preventing the play that she had written from being produced because she had not acceded to his sexual advances.

She had consequently withdrawn from the programme. She named the university as co-defendant in her five-hundred-thousand-dollar lawsuit. The university dismissed her claim, noting, among other things, that she had not used the university's complaints procedure while a student. Larry Elswit, associate general counsel at the university, pointed out that Walcott was only one of three professors who together decided which student plays should be produced.

Years later, in 2009, these charges were to be recalled to cast a shadow over Walcott's nomination for the position of professor of poetry at Oxford. He was the front-runner for the job, and his leading supporters included Hermione Lee, Alan Hollinghurst, Marina Warner and Robert Conquest. His main competitor was Ruth Padel. An anonymous smear campaign was begun against Walcott, by way of the circulation of the story of the sexual harassment charges that had been brought against him. Walcott withdrew from the candidacy, citing the low level to which the election had sunk. Padel was appointed. However, she soon resigned from the post, admitting that she had sent email messages to two newspaper reporters, calling their attention to the charges of sexual harassment against Walcott. She said that she had acted injudiciously, but without any animosity towards Walcott.[22] Interestingly, Nicole Niemi, under her married name Nicole Kelby, was quoted by the *Guardian* as being "appalled and saddened by the anonymous smear campaign against [her] former mentor, Derek Walcott".[23]

Walcott accepted an appointment as professor of poetry at the University of Essex shortly after the unfortunate end to his competing for the post of professor of poetry at Oxford.

Perhaps this is an opportune moment at which to take further note of Walcott's personality and temperament as they have appeared to those who have interacted with him over the years. We have already noted something of this earlier. It is a case of mutually opposing tendencies. In its report on his having won the Nobel Prize, the *Trinidad Guardian* quoted Norline, his third wife: "Underneath the façade of arrogance and strength, he is genuinely kind, gentle and sweet" (9 October 1992, 1). While some people have found him to be not outgoing, others have remarked "a gaiety about him, a love of banter".[24] On the one hand, he is thoughtful of others, generous, not self-promoting, not given to "talking shop", but with a delight in playful jabs, as much at himself as at his interlocutors. On the other hand, he can be unexpectedly, puzzlingly curt, sarcastic, dismissive, a reaction especially hurtful to those who approach him for the first time, after, say, a reading, out of their admiration for his work and in the expectation of having a pleasant exchange with him. The question may then be, how can they ever be sure that they will catch him in the right mood.

In a report on his reading in Kingston in April 2004, Sharon Leach wrote: "Walcott, who is known for his customary irascibility, responded affably, graciously, candidly and oftentimes with self-deprecating humour." She went on to report that, in answer to a question from the audience as to what the response to a good poetry reading should be, he "quipped [that] the only real 'reaction to good poetry is stunned boredom. . . . I've seen that tonight.' "[25] Perhaps the quip was not quite so "light-hearted" as she said it was.

※

During his Boston years, Walcott's output of poetry and plays increased steadily, enhancing his reputation. He was also in increasing demand for participation at literary events (readings, lectures, discussions) both within and outside the United States. His stock of honours and awards grew. In poetry, *The Fortunate Traveller* (1982) was followed by *Midsummer* (1984) and *The Arkansas Testament* (1987). In the 1990s came *Omeros* (1990) and *The Bounty* (1997), followed in the next decade by *Tiepolo's Hound* (2000) and *The Prodigal* (2004).

The Fortunate Traveller, the first collection published after he began to live in the United States, opens with a few poems in which he reflects on his view of the United States, his relationship with his new country of domicile – poems such as "Old New England", "American Muse" and "Piano Practice". The collection is arranged in three sections, "North", "South" and "North". The fact that "South" is framed by "North", so to speak, may be significant. This movement reflects the poet's travels, literally and in imagination, between south and north, between his island(s) and the wide world, between Third World and First World, as well as the North-South divide of the United States – all this from the point of view, at once self-deprecating and pointedly tongue-in cheek, of "a colonial upstart at the end of an empire" (*Fortunate*, 11).

One aspect of the problematics of location is the sense of

being in some way a stranger when he returns home. This sense is implicit in "The Hotel Normandie Pool". When Walcott visited Trinidad in his early Boston years, he would sometimes stay at the Normandie Hotel in Port of Spain. His daughters would visit him there and swim in the pool. The poet-persona, thinking about them and their mother, acknowledges "the disfiguring exile of divorce" (*Fortunate*, 65). One day another guest who comes to the pool, with sandals and a white towel slung over his shoulder like a toga, becomes, to the poet's imagination, the Roman poet Ovid. Walcott, calling to mind the demerits of the sociopolitical situation of the West Indies, finds that "corruption, censorship and arrogance / make exile seem a happier thought than home" (67).

The topos of the poet's journeying between home and abroad, with its ramifications and its concomitant engagement with self-scrutiny, is extended in *Midsummer* and *The Arkansas Testament*. The former opens with a poem about returning home, the poet's heart shuddering with emotion when the jet hits the tarmac as it lands at the airport in Trinidad. The presence of Joseph Brodsky threads through the book, evoking the theme of the poet in exile, and underscoring the poet-persona's faith that although he may die far from home, "the grateful grass [of home] will grow thick from his heart" (*Midsummer*, 74). Midsummer, the seasonal setting of all the places traversed in the book, is also a pervasive metaphor for the poet's fervid, fertile imagination.

The book gives the impression of being not so much a collection of diverse poems, but one long poem comprising units that each has its separate validity. This impression is underlined by the fact that the individual poems are all identified not by titles, but by Roman numerals in sequence. (Only three also have a title.) What is more, the sense of a unified whole is evident in the collection's control of form. The poems vary in length within a narrow range of seventeen to twenty-eight lines. The lines are long, a sort of loose pentameter, occasionally hexameter, of generally unemphatic stress and using occasional rhyme, often half-rhyme. The overall effect of the verse form enhances the mood of introspection, and of the unresting tide, the midsummer flare of the poetic imagination.

Walcott's exploration of the discipline of verse form, his pursuit of "more care in the craft of verse" is extended in *The Arkansas Testament* (176). Now there are mostly short-line poems, and most of these are in quatrains, almost all of them rhyming *abab*. The influence of W.H. Auden is evident, in a poet who has always been willing to practise and acknowledge his debt to the Old Masters of verse. The Audenesque "Eulogy to W.H. Auden" was read by Walcott at Auden's memorial service at the Cathedral of St John the Divine, New York City, on 17 October 1983.

The Arkansas Testament also extends the motif of the poet's journeying between home and abroad. Reminiscent of the "North"/"South"/"North" grouping of the poems in *Midsummer*, the poems in *The Arkansas Testament* are grouped in two sections, "Here" and Elsewhere", focusing the contrasts, tensions, synergy and similarity between the two "locations", and their connection with the poet's identity quest. In this regard, his response to the United States is elaborated in poems like "Winter Lamps" (which also evokes the breakdown of a marriage, presumably his own), "A Propertius Quartet", and, most tellingly, the title poem. One poem which has elicited high praise, "The Light of the World", is about the mixed feelings attendant on returning home. In counterpoint to his love of home, and his feeling of celebratory admiration of a woman whom he sees on a bus on which he is riding, is his guilty sense of a disconnection between himself and the people, a feeling of his having "abandoned them" (*Arkansas*, 51), of his being only a "transient" in his homeland. Ironically, the bus lets him off at the Halcyon Hotel, where he is staying during his visit – at home, but in a hotel; in a happy and peaceful place, but at odds with himself.

Omeros (1990) was a landmark new departure in Walcott's poetic odyssey, a development in the undertaking of a book-length narrative poem, a foray which he had begun with *Another Life*, and which has been a challenge to modern poets. Using as foundation and analogy *The Iliad,* he naturalizes Homer in a story that gives the St Lucian folk heroic voice even as they lose none of their real-life actuality as simple people. The naturalizing is enhanced by the poet's self-reflexive addressing of Homer. The modernizing of Homer also comes naturally in Walcott's free-ranging narrative, and in the novelization of epic.

Two outstanding features of the poem, advances in the journey of the poet's creative imagination, are, with regard to subject-matter, the new depth of attention to the African heritage of the West Indian people, and, with regard to form, the sustaining of the one, demanding verse form throughout (with only a brief, knowing departure), and that without any strain or rigidity. Achille's dream voyage across the Atlantic to meet his West African father redresses the romantic-nostalgic dream return of which Makak, in *Dream on Monkey Mountain*, had to disabuse himself. Alongside Achille's self-affirming reconnection is Ma Kilman and her journey into the forest, following the pull of ancestral folk culture and medicine, to find the plant that will heal Philoctete's wound. In respect of form, Walcott's use of terza rima, holding together the various turnings of content, with the masterful manipulation of rhyme not shouting for attention, is a large factor in the recognition which the poem has gained as one of the most successful modern book-length narrative poems, or, indeed, epics.

The year of *Omeros*'s publication, 1990, also brought grief, with the death of Walcott's mother, Alix, in May, at the age of ninety-five. Chapter 32 of *Omeros* is a seeming digression from the narrative plot, but luminous and heart-stopping. It recounts her son's visit with her, presumably his last, at the Marian Home for the Elderly, in Castries, where she lived in her last days. His memory of the allamanda and bougainvillea that beautified her house on Chaussee Road, his memory of the energy with which she worked at her sewing machine, counterpoints her present amnesia and her wisps of thinning white hair, to evoke the tensions that thread love, death and memory. His first new collection of poems to appear after her death, *The Bounty* (1997), opens with the title sequence, which is an elegy for her, and is dedicated "For Alix Walcott".

CHAPTER FOUR

The sequence, drawing on John Clare and Dante, and recognizing the nexus between personal and social concerns, signals the themes and tone that will inform the volume: the inexhaustible bounty of life, even in its smallest, seemingly most inconsequential things, a bounty over and against the realities of time and death, in the fact that we can find cause for "praise in decay and process, awe in the ordinary" (*Bounty*, 7).

The overall form, style and sound of *The Bounty* are akin to those of *Midsummer*, contributing likewise to the impression of a unified whole. Whereas the opening title-sequence is in terza rima, the rest of the book comprises poems ranging between eighteen and twenty-six lines, with all but four being between twenty and twenty-five. The lines are a kind of irregular iambic pentameter, usually of twelve syllables or more, and with low-key, irregular rhyming that constitutes "disguised" terza rima.

Following on *Omeros* and *Another Life*, *Tiepolo's Hound* and *The Prodigal* extend Walcott's experimentation with the book-length narrative poem. *Tiepolo's Hound* interweaves two stories. One is about Camille Pissarro, one of the founders of impressionist and post-impressionist painting, who was born on the island of St Thomas, in what was then the Danish West Indies, but who eventually settled in Paris in order to realize his artistic ambition. Alongside the Pissarro story, and speaking to it, is the story of the poet's quest to find again a painting, which he had once seen, in which there was a white hound with a radiant thigh, and to settle definitively whether the painting was by Tiepolo or Veronese.

Together the two stories extend Walcott's exploration of the relationship between painting and poetry, and his lifelong musing on his being drawn by the two. The book's poetry is Walcott's tribute to painting, a point underlined by the inclusion of twenty-six full-colour reproductions of his paintings, as well as by the fact that the back of the jacket reproduces a photograph of a young Walcott at his easel, and wearing, fittingly, a broad-brimmed straw hat. Appropriately, too, the book is dedicated to Sigrid, thereby acknowledging her own career in art.

The two stories between them comprehend some others of Walcott's pervasive themes, such as: the North-South dialogue, the tensions and parallels between home and abroad, the Caribbean artist/poet and his or her relationship to Europe, the legacy of colonialism and its factors of ethnicity and race.

In *Tiepolo's Hound*, Walcott furthers his inventiveness in modulating traditional verse forms to sustain and unify a long, free-ranging narrative poem. Now there is a disciplined interweaving of couplet and quatrain. The lines, of flexible iambic pentameter, are set on the page in unrhymed couplets, but each successive pair of couplets forms a quatrain rhyming unemphatically *abab*. At the end of the book, in the interface of the two narrative sequences, Pissarro's death, in Paris, occurs just as the poet returns home. The poem ends with a benediction that redeems "the repeated failures, the botched trepidations" (163) of Pissarro and Walcott.

The Prodigal (2004) is Walcott's ultimate homecoming poem. The book is in three parts, comprising eighteen numbered "chapters" (no titles) each divided into three, four or five subsections or poems. In this structure it broadly resembles *Tiepolo's Hound* and *Omeros*, as also in the sustaining of one verse form throughout – in this instance a loose blank verse, sometimes almost sliding into free verse. A similar kind of sustaining form was to function in *White Egrets* (2010), but now, with a pervasive use of rhyme, and a more lyrical mode, one may think in terms of variations on the sonnet.

With its informing analogy to the biblical story of the prodigal son, *The Prodigal* brings to a kind of culmination, though not to an end, Walcott's theme of journey, his exploration of the tensions and energizing force of his continual movement between island and world, between "Here" and "Elsewhere", in his quest for identity. In this quest, the idea of the interplay between word and world is dynamic. So, for instance, the Hudson's flow is "narrative" (*Prodigal*, 6), and the poem opens: "In autumn, on the train to Pennsylvania, / he placed his book face-down on the sunlit seat / and it began to move" (3).

When he asks himself, "Prodigal, what were your wanderings about?" (70), the question refers not only to his actual geographical movements from his home-place out into and across the world, but even more significantly to the journeys of his imagination across landscapes, cultures and history. He is now based in St Lucia, but his return does not mean cessation of the quest, and the celebration of his native landscape is resonant with other landscapes through which he has passed. With the sense of having come full circle, he even tells himself that *The Prodigal* is "what will be [his] last book" (99). That assertion, we suspect, is really rhetorical, demanded by the truth of the poem's fiction. At the end of the poem he is still travelling, albeit dolphin-watching on a boat off the coast of St Lucia; but this voyage acquires a visionary transfiguration. The dolphins, rising in the air, suggest the radiance of angels.

FIVE

In theatre, between 1981 and 1986 there were no fewer than six premieres. In April 1981, *Beef, No Chicken* was staged at the Little Carib Theatre, with Cecil Gray directing the Trinidad Theatre Workshop. This was Walcott's successful foray into farce, with social criticism as its aim. The plot centres on a project to build a modern highway through the small town of Couva in Trinidad. The play's target of social criticism is the euphoria over a "development" that means concrete and the destruction of the natural environment. A few of the workshop's foremost actors had leading parts: Errol Jones, Stanley Marshall, Claude Reid. The play was then produced by the Yale Repertory Theatre in New Haven Connecticut in January–February 1982, under the direction of Walton Jones, with an American cast.

In April 1982, Douglas Turner Ward and his Negro Ensemble Company, in collaboration with the Hartford Stage Company, presented *The Isle Is Full of Noises* at the Huntington Theatre in Hartford, Connecticut. This play undertakes an all-encompassing view, through the lens of sociopolitical criticism and satire, of the colonial and postcolonial history of the West Indies, the contemporary corruption and hunger for power that it has spawned, and the attempt to make a revolutionary break from them. The title, taken from Shakespeare's *The Tempest*, hints at the play's subject-matter. The play, laden with characters, appeared sprawling and self-indulgent. It was never published.[26]

July 1982 saw the first production of *The Last Carnival*, directed by the playwright, at the Government Training Centre in Port of Spain. With Walcott no longer working with the Trinidad Theatre Workshop, this production was presented by Warwick Productions. It was also staged in June 1983 by the Group Theatre Company of Seattle, Washington, directed by Reuben Sierra. The play covers the same general thematic area as *The Isle Is Full of Noises* and *Beef, No Chicken*, but now by focusing on the failed attempt at revolution in Trinidad and Tobago in 1970. It may be read as Walcott revisiting, indirectly, his view of the situation at the time. Its fiction dramatizes the tension and interaction between Trinidad's French Creole upper class and the blacks who seek to overturn the sociopolitical status quo. The play undertakes a questioning, balanced view of things, although, in the process, it somewhat emasculates the would-be revolutionaries.

In November 1983, *A Branch of the Blue Nile*, directed by Earl Warner, was first produced, by Stage One and the Nation Publishing Company at Stage One in Bridgetown, Barbados. This play is very much about theatre, about its pull and challenges for actor and director, about the actor's life and commitment. More particularly, it is about the challenge of developing a sustainable, fully realized West Indian theatre, whose West Indianness will not exclude engagement with the Classics, Shakespeare, Western theatre. The play brings to mind Walcott's experience with the Trinidad Theatre Workshop, but is not narrowly limited to that experience in an autobiographical way. The production was well received. Major roles were played by Walcott's then wife, Norline Metivier (Marilyn), and Michael Gilkes, the Guyanese director, actor, playwright and poet (Christopher).

Also in 1983 there was the broadcast, on television in Trinidad and Tobago, of a made-for-television film, written and directed by Walcott and produced by Bruce Paddington's Banyan Productions. *The Rig* (title ironic) is another instance of Walcott's sociopolitical criticism, another comment on so-called development. It is also a notable expression of Walcott's career-long aspiration in film-writing and production. Through a story of intrigue and shenanigans, the film deals with the questionable impact on society of the discovery of oil off the east coast of Trinidad.

Cinema has had a pervasive influence on Walcott's imagination as a writer, an influence that has been carefully studied by Jean Antoine-Dunne.[27] He wrote film scripts, and drew storyboards for them, some accessible or partially accessible only in Walcott archives. As early as 1972 there was an agreement for a film titled *Vangelo Nero* to be produced by Produzioni De Laurentiis. The film project on which he worked most assiduously over decades, for which he garnered much footage, but which remains uncompleted, is a movie version of *Ti-Jean and His Brothers*. In the essay "Down the

Coast",[28] he retraces this venture, his regret balanced by elation.

In August 1984, Walcott directed, for the Government of St Lucia, at the Morne, Castries, his *The Haitian Earth*, to commemorate the one hundred and fiftieth anniversary of emancipation. Set design was by Richard Montgomery, with costumes by Sally Montgomery. The cast included some of St Lucia's most highly regarded actors, such as Arthur Jacobs, Gandolph St Clair and McDonald Dixon. Norline Metivier played the role of Yette. The play revisits a subject of two of Walcott's most path-finding early works, *Henri Christophe* and *Drums and Colours*. Now, though, the focus is not on the "hero", the individual with the will to seize and wield power, but on the unsung heroism of the common people, the folk.

In October 1986, *To Die for Grenada* opened at the Cleveland Playhouse. This play, which did not get good reviews, engaged with the Grenada Revolution of 1979 and the 1983 American invasion of Grenada which brought it to an end. The play was never published.

Of the next six plays, four were set outside the Caribbean. In November 1989, *The Ghost Dance*, commissioned by Hartwick College, Oneonta, for its Cardboard Alley Players, was staged there, directed by Duncan Smith and designed by Richard and Sally Montgomery. The historical story with which this play deals is one that would have been of immediate appeal to the Walcott who had previously written, in his poetry, about the near-extermination of the Native American. The play tells the story of Catherine Weldon, a white widow from Brooklyn, who went to the Sioux reservation to help

CHAPTER FIVE

the Sioux to resist the attempt of the government to take their land from them. She undertook to be the secretary and agent of their chief, Sitting Bull. Their effort failed, but she returned to join Sitting Bull's camp. She tried, unsuccessfully, to persuade him not to persist with a ritual called the Ghost Dance, lest it be used by the government as an excuse to jail and kill him. This attempt also failed. Weldon and the Ghost Dance were also to feature in *Omeros*, in what might mistakenly be seen as a digression, but is really an illuminating sidelight on the main story of the poem.

In June 1990, *Viva Detroit* had its world premiere at the Los Angeles Theatre Center. The fact that this play, a comedy, has not been published may be connected with its lukewarm reception. It was directed by Claude Purdy, with a three-person cast: Robert Gossett, Moses Gunn and Gates McFadden. Despite what its title may suggest, the play is very much about St Lucia and the Caribbean. It deals with the ill-effects of the tourist industry on small islands like St Lucia, an issue that had long attracted Walcott's passionate disfavour. In her review for the *Los Angeles Times* (11 June 1990), Sylvie Drake said that, although the direction was energetic, the characters were superficial and the plot not well developed nor resolved.

In May 1991, *Steel*, a musical, with music by Galt MacDermot and set by Richard Montgomery, was staged, under the direction of Walcott and Robert Scanlan, as part of the Philadelphia American Music Theater Festival, at Plays and Players Theatre. It had previewed at the end of April at the Hasty Pudding theatre at Harvard. It tells the story of the development of the steel band in its early years, with a fictional romantic relationship interwoven. In the process, it also engages with various public issues of the time, both local and international. Reviewers found the plot too diffuse and difficult to follow, and the characters, of which there are many, not clearly realized. However, the music was very well received. The reaction was basically the same when a revised version of the play was staged by the Trinidad Theatre Workshop at Queen's Hall, Port of Spain, in September 2005. On this occasion, a few of the actors were praised.

In 1992 came *The Odyssey: A Stage Version*, presented, to acclaim, by the Royal Shakespeare Company at the Other Place, Stratford-upon-Avon, and directed by Gregory Doran. It moved to London in 1993. Complementing *Omeros*, Walcott's play modernizes and "Caribbeanizes" Homer, and gives the story a theatrical integrity by way of omissions, additions and changes of emphasis. To cite just one instance, he introduces a narrator, Billy Blue, a blind blues singer (blind Homer entering the story, so to speak). The forward movement of the play is enhanced by the fact that the dialogue consists almost entirely of speeches no more than one line long, in contrast with the sometimes very long speeches in Homer's epics. In October 1994, the play was produced at the Fichandler Stage at the Arena Stage Theatre in Washington, DC.

In December 1993, *Walker*, commissioned by the Boston Athenaeum, was produced as an opera, for one performance only, with libretto by Walcott and music by T.J. Anderson. A revised version, with music by Galt MacDermot, was staged by the Boston Playwrights Theatre in November 2001. Like

CHAPTER FIVE

The Ghost Dance, Walker is a non-Caribbean play by Walcott whose subject has a natural, strong appeal to his Caribbean world-view, and both plays increase the visibility of events in the history of the United States that are not widely known. *Walker* imagines the last few, fateful hours of David Walker, an early nineteenth-century African American freedman, who advocated violent uprising by the slaves against their masters.

Another musical, *Capeman*, by Paul Simon, with libretto by Walcott and Simon, opened at the Marquis Theatre, Broadway in January 1998. Walcott had finally reached Broadway, but disappointingly so. The production went through an uncomfortable gestation, with three changes of director, and Walcott was not happy about changes to his lyrics. Although the production received Tony Award nominations, it got mainly poor reviews and closed after two months. It told the story of Salvador Agrón, a young Puerto Rican gang member, convicted of murdering two teenagers in New York. A much shorter, better received version was staged at Central Park's Delacorte Theater in the summer of 2010.

In 1986 Walcott was awarded a Gold Musgrave Medal by the Institute of Jamaica for eminence in the field of Literature. He was presented with the medal at a ceremony at the Institute in May 1988, when he visited Jamaica to be the keynote speaker at the eighth annual conference on West Indian literature, held at the Mona campus of the University of the West Indies. His paper, titled "Caligula's Horse",[29] was engagingly provocative, chiding literary critics and theorists for their demands on poetry. He also read, for the first time to any audience, extracts from the long poem he was then working on, the poem that would turn out to be *Omeros*.

From Kingston to London. In June 1988 he was presented with the Queen's Gold Medal for Poetry, he being the first Commonwealth citizen ever to receive it. Sigrid and Anna accompanied him to Buckingham Palace for the presentation by Her Majesty. They did not actually witness the presentation, but while they waited in an anteroom, they had the pleasure of being chatted to briefly by the Queen's consort, His Royal Highness Prince Philip, who had come into the room to hear the score in a cricket match that was being broadcast.

In 1990 Walcott received an honorary doctorate from Hartwick College, Oneonta, New York, where *The Ghost Dance* had had its premiere in 1989. In 1990, *Omeros*, drawing on Homer's *Iliad* to configure a Caribbean epic of the St Lucian folk, was published, and boosted significantly his international reputation. In 1991 it won him Britain's W.H. Smith Literary Award, and was the decisive factor in his winning the Nobel Prize for Literature in 1992. In May 1991, he gave a reading at the Olivier Theatre, the National Theatre, London, and in June delivered a lecture on "The Legacy of Europe" at the International Writers Conference, Dublin.

The year 1992 was a stellar one for Walcott, and not just because of the Nobel Prize and *The Odyssey: A Stage Verson*. He also became one of the first three awardees of the Order of the Caribbean Community, given to "Caribbean nationals whose legacy in the economic, political, social and cultural

CHAPTER FIVE

metamorphoses of Caribbean society is phenomenal". Then there was a joyful family landmark, the marriage of daughter Lizzie to landscaping engineer David Hackshaw, on 4 October, at St Ann's Church, Port of Spain. Derek flew down from Boston to give his daughter's hand in marriage. At the reception they danced to one of Paul Simon's songs, "The Coast", which Simon had dedicated to his friend.

It was shortly after his return to Boston that Walcott received a telephone call, on the morning of 8 October, telling him that he had been awarded the Nobel Prize. One of the first things he did was telephone his ex-wife Margaret in Trinidad to share the news. Soon he was bombarded by reporters and photographers. He went to have breakfast at Dunkin Donuts. He told the Reuters reporter, "The principal thing is that West Indian literature has been recognized internationally, and that's good."[30]

On 17 November he arrived in St Lucia to a hero's welcome. Among those meeting him at the airport was his sister, Pam, who had flown in from Barbados. He was taken from the airport to Columbus Square, where a crowd, including groups of schoolchildren, was awaiting him. There was a programme of readings from his works; music was provided by the police band. The event was filmed by a Swedish film crew, which had come to St Lucia to make a documentary of the laureate's return home. They also filmed him visiting Pigeon Island and Patience Estate, and filmed bits from *Omeros*, dramatized on beaches of the island's west coast. He was awarded the national honour of the St Lucia Cross.

In the previous week in November, the Department of

English and the Institute of Caribbean Studies at the University of the West Indies' Mona campus in Jamaica, had presented "An Evening of Tributes and Readings" in Walcott's honour, at the Philip Sherlock Centre for the Creative Arts. Among those giving tributes was Sir Philip Sherlock, himself a poet, former vice chancellor of the university, who had, as was noted earlier, known Walcott and been impressed by his promise during his years as a student on the campus.

In December, the Trinidad Theatre Workshop celebrated Walcott with a concert at the Old Fire Station downtown Port of Spain, their temporary home. The theatre space, named the Wilbert Holder Room, was refurbished for the occasion. Wayne Brown, Patricia Ismond, Laurence Goldstraw and others read Walcott poems. Trinidad Theatre Workshop actors performed extracts from *Dream on Monkey Mountain*, *The Joker of Seville*, *Pantomime* and *Ti-Jean and His Brothers*. Walcott had helped with the scene painting, and took his impromptu turn at the drums with the musical accompaniment. At the end of the concert he was given a standing ovation.

Also in December, the Faculty of Arts and General Studies of the University of the West Indies at St Augustine presented, at the J.F.K. Auditorium, "The Living Word", a tribute to the Nobel laureate.

In January 1993, St Lucia inaugurated Nobel Laureate Week, an annual celebration of the island's two Nobel laureates, Derek Walcott and Sir Arthur Lewis (economics, 1979), who, *mirabile dictu*, shared the same birthday, 23 January. In that first Nobel Laureate Week, Columbus Square

CHAPTER FIVE

was renamed Derek Walcott Square, and on 29 January there was "An Evening with Derek Walcott" at the National Cultural Centre. This featured a reading by Walcott, and extracts from his plays, staged by a St Lucia Drama Group and the Trinidad Theatre Workshop.

Characteristically, Walcott also set in motion two initiatives that would use some of the money from the prize to assist with the development of creative arts in the Caribbean. These were the Rat Island Foundation and the James Rodway Memorial Prize for Poetry. The Rat Island Foundation would facilitate the establishment of an artists' retreat and mentoring centre on Rat Island, a three-acre islet off the north-western coast of St Lucia. However, the foundation never really got off the ground. The James Rodway Memorial Prize for Poetry was named in honour of Walcott's early mentor and promoter. Rodway had died just two weeks before that first Nobel Laureate Week, on 12 January 1993. The prize was awarded twice: in 1994 to James Christopher Aboud of Trinidad and Tobago, and in 1995 to Jane King of St Lucia.

In April 1993, Walcott, visiting Jamaica for the "Gathering of Graduates" at the University of the West Indies, Mona, was presented with one of Jamaica's highest national honours, the Order of Merit. The presentation was made by the governor general, Sir Howard Cooke. The distinguished individuals present included the prime minister of Jamaica, P.J. Patterson, and the prime minister of Barbados, Erskine Sandiford.

A more long-lasting material product of the Nobel Prize for Walcott was personal. It enabled him to build a house in St Lucia, the house that was to become his home in his late years. The house is idyllically located at Becune Point, Cap Estate, a fairly wooded, secluded area at the northern tip of the island, a short distance from Gros Islet. From the patio, one looks out over the swimming pool, over the cliff, and across the inlet, to Pigeon Island. The first part of the residence to be completed was a guest cottage to one side of the main house. Walcott and Sigrid moved into it in 1994, and stayed there from time to time to oversee the building of the main house, which they began to occupy in 1997. To the other side of the main house, semi-detached, is a well-designed studio, where Walcott painted, and where he also wrote on his manual Olivetti typewriter. From the house it is a short drive to the beach at Rodney Bay, where he would swim every morning and snack on grilled fish, grilled chicken and "bake".

At the sixth Caribbean Festival of Arts (Carifesta), held in Trinidad and Tobago in August 1995, Walcott was the main attraction among the nine Caribbean writers honoured. Some of his works were performed: Che Rodriguez and the Trinidad Theatre Workshop danced to "The Light of the World" set to music; Errol Jones and Stanley Marshall acted an extract from *Dream on Monkey Mountain*.

In May 1996, Walcott gave a lecture at the Caribana Milano Conference at the University of Milan, and in March 1998 Artistic Expressions Limited presented a reading by Walcott at the Crowne Plaza Hotel in Kingston, Jamaica. In November of the same year Warwick University in England conferred on him an honorary doctor of letters degree, and he did a reading of his poetry at the Warwick Arts Centre. In 1999, it was reported that Walcott was being considered for appointment as poet laureate of England, and that he was not averse to the idea. He was quoted as saying, "To follow in the footsteps of Tennyson, Masefield, C. Day Lewis and Betjeman sends a shiver down my spine."[31]

The twenty-first century opened with new grief for Walcott. On 6 March his brother Roderick died in Toronto, where he had been living for some time. Derek was in Mexico at the time and there was some delay in contacting him. In *The Prodigal* (50), Walcott records the impact of the news with a segue from factual directness to emotionally evocative, figurative indirectness:

> I read this.
> March 11, 8.35 a.m. Guadalajara, Saturday.
> Roddy. Toronto. Cremated today.
> The streets and trees of Mexico covered with ash.
> Your soul, my twin, keeps fluttering in my head,
> a hummingbird, bewildered by the rafters . . . .

Roddy was buried in Choc Cemetery, where his mother, who had died ten years earlier, is also buried: "no lights at dusk on the short street / where my brother and our mother live now / at the one address, so many are their neighbours!" (51). In November 2011, the Open Campus of the University of the West Indies hosted Roderick Walcott Week in Castries, in recognition of his work as one of the founders of modern Caribbean theatre. Derek and Sigrid were present. To balance the grief of Roddy's death, there was cause for family celebration the following year, when, on 7 January 2001, Anna married Mark Hardy, an aeronautical engineer.

The Nobel laureate continued to be in transatlantic demand in his seventies, and his list of honours and awards continued to grow. In September 2000 he was featured at the Great Salt Lake Book Festival in Salt Lake City, where he gave a reading from *Tiepolo's Hound* and was interviewed on stage. In 2001–2003 he conducted a series of summer seminars at the University of Milan on the initiative of Professor Luigi Sampietro. In March 2004 he did a reading at the twentieth-anniversary celebration of the Centre for Caribbean Studies, University of Warwick. In the following month, Artistic Expressions Limited presented him in a reading at the Hilton Kingston hotel in Jamaica. In 2004 he also received the Anisfield-Wolf Book Award for Lifetime Achievement, given for books "that make an important contribution to the understanding of racism and the rich diversity of human culture".

On 27 April 2005, Walcott took part in "Season of Laureates: Readings in Honor of the Seventieth Birthday of Wole Soyinka", hosted by the W.E.B. Du Bois Institute, Harvard. The programme was chaired by Henry Louis Gates Jr, and the other Nobel laureates reading to the overflow audience were Nadine Gordimer and Toni Morrison. Walcott read excerpts from *The Odyssey: A Stage Version*. Then, in July–August, by arrangement with Change Performing Arts of Milan, he took the play on a European tour: to the Ortigia Festival in Syracuse, Sicily; to the Caserta Festival; and to the Merida Festival in Spain. The script was a collage of four

CHAPTER FIVE

languages: standard English, Italian, Castilian and St Lucian Creole, with the translation of Walcott's text into Italian and Spanish done by Matteo Campagnoli. The cast comprised Europeans and West Indians, including Antonio Varelo (Ulysses), Giovanna Bozzola (Penelope), Brian Green, Albert Laveau, Arthur Jacobs, Eunice Wright.

St Lucian journalist Jason Sifflet, who was a member of the cast, published in the St Lucia *Star* in seven instalments, between 4 July and 24 August 2005, his account of the experience of working under Walcott's direction. He highlights how hard Walcott drives the actors, and on what can seem puzzling, disconcerting, even infuriating in his method. Sifflet's account is well summed up in the title of the report, "The Wrath of Walcott", and in his phrase "benevolent tyranny".[32]

Later that year, on 18 November, an exhibition of his paintings, captioned *Another Life*, opened at the June Kelly Gallery in New York City. It was his first solo exhibition. In a review for the *New York Times* (26 November 2005), Ken Johnson wrote that Walcott "is more of a devoted hobbyist than a painter".

In April 2006, he read at Vassar College, New York. In June the degree of honorary doctor of letters was conferred on him by Oxford University. Before that he was awarded the Premio Grinzane Cavour in Turin. He also received an honorary doctorate from the University of Urbino in the same year, and there was a performance in Italian of *The Odyssey: A Stage Version*. In September 2007 he was the Mark Flanagan Distinguished Writer at the University of Calgary. In October, as Janet Weiss Fellow in Contemporary Letters at Bucknell University, he read a selection of his poems and answered questions from the audience.

On 2 December 2007, Elizabeth Hardwick, Robert Lowell's widow, died. Walcott was unable to attend her memorial service in New York City on 16 December, but his tribute to her was read by Hilton Als of the *New Yorker*. Walcott described with warm acuity distinctive aspects of her character and talent. He recalled happy times shared by their two families decades earlier, his, with second wife Margaret and his son, Peter, and hers, with husband Robert Lowell and their daughter, Harriet.

Walcott retired from Boston University in 2007.

SIX

As he moved into his eighties, Walcott's creativity in playwriting and directing continued to be as productive as his poetry, and to take fresh turns. At the same time, there came a deepening sense of ending, a sense at once balanced and underscored by a sequence of celebrations of his lifetime of achievement.

In May 2009, Walcott set foot on African soil for the first time. The occasion was not literary. On the initiative of Wole Soyinka (1986 Nobel laureate), he was among a group of eminent people who met in Lagos to take part in the Food Security and Poverty Alleviation Conference. In 1997 Walcott had been one of many signatories, all Nobel laureates in literature, to an open letter to the editors of the *New York Review of Books* (24 April 1997), protesting the Nigerian government's condemning Soyinka to death for alleged treason. Walcott's participation in a programme of readings at Harvard in 2005, in celebration of Soyinka's seventieth birthday, was noted in the preceding chapter. St Lucians welcomed Soyinka rousingly in 2010, when he gave the Derek Walcott Nobel Lecture to mark Walcott's eightieth birthday.

The year 2010 also opened with loss, the death of Walcott's sister, Pam (Mrs Leonard St Hill), in Barbados, where she had lived most of her life. Her memorial service was held at the James Street Methodist Church, Bridgetown. Her body was cremated and the ashes interred in Choc cemetery at Vigie, where her mother, Alix, and her brother Roddy already lay. Derek and Sigrid were present at the interment. He was now the last surviving member of the Chaussee Road family.

In the same year, his poetic creativity continued to make its mark, with the publication of *White Egrets*. The egrets, after whom the book and its title poem/sequence are named, and which "speckle the islands / on river-bank, in mangrove marsh or cattle pasture" (7), are particularly associated in Walcott's mind with Trinidad's Santa Cruz valley, where his daughters have lived since the early 2000s. They had houses built there side-by-side, on Santa Barbara Boulevard, with no fence between them, in an idyllic setting: a wide expanse of lawn, with lush vegetation backing the lawn, and the egrets from time to time. Santa Cruz had featured in *The Prodigal* (chapter 12) and before that in *The Bounty* ("A Santa Cruz Quartet").

White Egrets continued his pursuit of some of his major themes, such as the journeying between island and world, the dialogue between "Here" and "Elsewhere". We need only note some of the titles: "Sicilian Suite", "Spanish Series", "In Italy", "Barcelona", "In Amsterdam", "In Capri", "A London Afternoon", "In the Village" (that is, Greenwich Village). As we might expect, in this context the "world" is the Western world, and that mostly Europe. There are also the themes of

CHAPTER SIX

the role of place and landscape in self-realization, the confrontation of the imperial/colonial legacy, the interface of word and world, the attempt to come to terms with his never-quite-fulfilled ambition as a painter.

Through all of these, the dominant mood is valedictory, and the informing theme is that of ageing, and the illness and physical decay that come with it, signalling death: "dimming eyesight", "the quiet ravages of diabetes" (*White Egrets*, 6), "my hand trembles wildly" (47). There are the friends who have died, now memorialized: August Wilson ("6"); Oliver Jackman, Barbadian diplomat and writer ("7"); John Hearne ("41"), and Trinidad Theatre Workshop actors Wilbert Holder, Claude Reid and Ermine Wright ("37"). (Errol Jones was to die in June 2010, and Stanley Marshall in October 2013, both aged eighty-eight.) A most poignant landmark moment in the poet's life is recorded in "Sixty Years After", when, in the departure lounge at Hewanorra Airport, in St Lucia, he meets his first love, the Anna of *Another Life*. They are both in wheelchairs, she "hunched like a crumpled flower", "treble-chinned, old, her devastating / smile netted in wrinkles" (58). They are both, ironically, travelling.

However, the awareness of age, decay and impending death in *White Egrets* is not steeped in ruefulness and regret. Rather, it is deepened by acceptance, contentment and peace of mind, gratitude for what has been achieved, for the beneficence of life, for renewal and radiance – all these symbolized by the egrets. So he can say to himself, near the end of the book,

> Be happy now at Cap, for the simplest joys –
> for a line of white egrets prompting the last word,

for the sea's recitation re-entering my head
with questions it erases . . . .

(*White Egrets*, 63)

To turn to Walcott and the theatre in his eighties: on 4 April 2011, his *Moon-Child*, a musical based on *Ti-Jean and His Brothers*, was presented at the American Academy in Rome, in a staged reading, with music by Ronald "Boo" Hinkson and Andre Tanker. Walcott himself read the part of the Narrator, with Wendell Manwarren playing the Planter, Giovanna Bozzolo the Mother, and Dean Atta the Bolom. Artwork for the set was painted by Walcott and his son Peter. Later that month, on 30 April, the musical had its UK premiere at the Lakeside Theatre, University of Essex. Manwarren and Atta were again in the cast, but now Glyn Maxwell was the Narrator. The play received a standing ovation. In October 2012, there was a staged reading of *Dream on Monkey Mountain* by the Classical Theatre of Harlem, to accompany Walcott's keynote address for the symposium "Caribbean: Crossroads of the World", presented by El Museo del Barrio and the Studio Museum of Harlem.

In 2012, while at Essex, he began to write *O Starry, Starry Night*, which had its world premiere, also at the Lakeside, in May 2013. This play, whose title echoes the title of one of Vincent Van Gogh's most famous paintings, "The Starry Night", explores the friendship between Van Gogh and Paul Gauguin, concentrating on the few weeks they spent together in Arles. The play extends Walcott's interest in painting and its relationship with poetry. It also broached the idea of the tropics, the Caribbean, as world catalysts of art. Here too, Walcott promoted the international presence of Caribbean actors. All but one member of the cast were Trinidadian, including, notably, two of Walcott's Trinidad Theatre Workshop leading lights: Wendell Manwarren (Gauguin) and Nigel Scott (Theo).

In early April, Walcott invited the actors to his home in St Lucia, where he began rehearsing the play. He should have returned to Essex to take them through the last stages of rehearsal. However, his return was delayed when he suffered a stroke. In his absence, direction was taken over by the artistic director of the theatre, Barbara Peirson. Walcott did arrive in time for opening night.

Then came the production of *O Starry, Starry Night!* at Samaans' Park, St Lucia, in August of the same year, most of the cast being the same as for the Essex premiere. In November, it was Trinidad's turn, with the play being staged at the Central Bank Auditorium. True to his proactive concern for support for the development of the arts in the Caribbean, Walcott arranged for two members of the cast, David Tarkenter and Michael Prokopiou, to conduct an actors' workshop for students of the University of the West Indies and the University of Trinidad and Tobago. He also made it known that any profits from the production would go towards providing scholarships to students of theatre arts at the St Augustine campus of the University of the West Indies. Consequently, at a ceremony held at the campus on 24 December 2015, he presented the Derek Walcott Bursary, for 2014 and 2015, to two undergraduate students in the campus's Department of Festival and Creative Arts.

In May–June 2014, Walcott's stage adaptation of *Omeros*, directed by Bill Buckhurst, with music and sound effects by Tayo Abinkode, had its world premiere at the Sam Wanamaker Playhouse, the Globe Theatre, London. It was a remarkable achievement for Buckhurst, with Walcott's collaboration, to rework the multi-character epic poem into a play for two actors and a musician (Akinbode), with the two actors bringing to life the range of characters. The actors were Jade Anouka and Joseph Marcell. The latter, born in St Lucia, had made his name as an actor in England, popularly known for his role as the Butler in the television series *The Fresh Prince of Belair*.

According to J.D. Douglas, St Lucian-born author and producer, the idea of the adaptation began to take effect in a bar in Dennery, the night before the opening of the Globe's staging of *King Lear* in St Lucia, with Marcell in the lead role. Tom Bird, the Globe's executive producer, asked Douglas if he thought that Walcott might be interested in a staged reading of the poem. When asked, Walcott replied that he would be more interested in a staged production with music. At lunch at Walcott's house, with Douglas and Marcell also present, Buckhurst began to run ideas by Walcott as to the shape of the adaptation.[33]

A significant challenge was to decide what bits of the poem could be omitted. Buckhurst was also guided by sketches and watercolours which Walcott had done to illustrate the poem. Walcott later sent him a storyboard for the adaptation while

CHAPTER SIX

the play was in rehearsal. Buckhurst and the actors benefited greatly from these, many of which were mounted on the walls during rehearsals. The play was so well received that it was re-staged at the Globe in October 2015, with Joan Iyiola replacing Jade Anouka. Meanwhile, in May 2015, the Globe took it on tour to St Lucia. It was staged at the National Cultural Centre, as part of the twenty-fifth anniversary celebrations of the St Lucia Jazz and Arts Festival.

Walcott's entry into his eighties also saw, as has been pointed out earlier, a sequence of celebrations for his lifetime of achievement. In January 2010, to mark his eightieth birthday, the Department of Liberal Arts at the University of the West Indies, St Augustine campus, honoured him with a conference on the theme "Interlocking Basins of the Globe". There was also a panel discussion on Walcott's work as theatre director, featuring noted actors of the Trinidad Theatre Workshop. A special attraction was an exhibition of seventeen paintings by Walcott (fifteen watercolours and two oils) as well as a pleasantly surprising extra, Warwick Walcott's *Coconut Trees*, the watercolour of the coconut grove at Vigie mentioned in "On Leaving School". These paintings were from the collection of his daughters, Elizabeth and Anna, and their mother, Margaret.

In May 2013, to celebrate Walcott on the world premiere of his *O Starry, Starry Night!* at the University of Essex, Glyn Maxwell organized and chaired a programme of a selection of Walcott's poems, recited by the ensemble "Live Canon" and interspersed with readings of some of Walcott's favourite poems by other poets. Walcott was also honoured at the sixteenth triennial conference of the Association for Commonwealth Literature and Language Studies, held in St Lucia at the Sandals Grande hotel in August 2013. He was the subject of an onstage discussion with Edward Baugh. A most welcome "side show" was the staging of *O Starry, Starry Night!*, directed by Walcott himself, and with most of the cast from the Essex premiere.

In 2015 (April/May), to mark his eighty-fifth birthday, Trinidad and Tobago's Bocas Literary Festival paid tribute to Walcott with a special programme of events, chief of which was a tribute by various close associates of Walcott. This event, part of the Bocas Prize ceremony, was held at the Old Fire Station, once home to the Trinidad Theatre Workshop, and celebrated Walcott as the first winner of the Bocas Prize, in 2011, for *White Egrets*.

The festival also featured a panel discussion on the topic "Walcott vs Brathwaite?" and a series of films: documentaries on him, interviews with him, and films of his works. These included *The Rig*, mentioned earlier, and *Dream on Monkey Mountain*, directed by Hugh Robertson for National Broadcasting Company television in the US and broadcast in 1970. The documentaries included one of conversations between Walcott and Raoul Pantin, which had been televised in the early 1990s.

In May 2015, St Mary's College marked the one hundred and twenty-fifth anniversary of its founding. Walcott joined the large gathering of past and present students, parents, teachers and well-wishers at the commemorative service at the Minor Basilica in Castries. He sat for his photograph in

CHAPTER SIX

Walcott Square, with a few of the present students standing behind him, all, including the laureate, in white shirts.

In June 2015, Canada's Griffin Trust for Excellence in Poetry presented its Lifetime Achievement Award to Walcott. He was unable to attended the presentation ceremony, at which trustees Colm Tóibín and Michael Ondaatje each read one of Walcott's poems. On 21 November, the trust's executive director, Ruth Smith, presented the award to Walcott at his home in St Lucia.

Also in 2015, a group of theatre lovers in Port of Spain formed an ad hoc organization, "Monkey Mountain", to commemorate Walcott's achievement in theatre. They presented a sequence of three of his plays at the Little Carib Theatre: *Ti-Jean and His Brothers* in May, *Beef, No Chicken* in July, and *O Babylon!* in November.

Then, on 5 October 2015, it was the Boston Playwrights' Theatre's turn to celebrate Walcott, its founder. At the event, friends, former colleagues and students spoke about their experience of working with him. They shared anecdotes, including some about his off-the-cuff jokes, and read extracts from their own works and his. The programme was chaired by Kate Snodgrass, artistic director of the theatre, who had been Walcott's student in 1987–1988. The printed programme for the event included tributes to him by former students, such as Russell Lees and Anita Patterson. Distinguished participants included Wendell Manwarren, who came up from Trinidad for the occasion and sang a solo from *The Joker of Seville*. Walcott was unable to attend, but the evening was alive with his presence, and participant after participant spoke to him as if he were there. It was a moving expression of friendship, respect and admiration.

The wheel came full circle as it were, when, in January 2016, in Nobel Laureate Week, Walcott was honoured by the first school he attended, and the house in which he spent his childhood and youth was officially opened as Walcott House, a museum. The Methodist Infant School on Chisel Street, just "round the corner" from the Walcott home on Chaussee Road, had been amalgamated in 2002 with the Methodist Primary School, also originally on Chisel Street. The amalgamated institution was named the Gordon and Walcott Memorial Methodist School. "Gordon" was Thomas Doddridge Gordon, first head teacher of the primary school, while "Walcott" was, of course, Derek's mother Alix, the first head teacher of the infant school. The two schools had been relocated from Chisel Street to Darling Road. Other special guests at the celebration, apart from Derek and Sigrid, were retired judge Michael Gordon, grandson of T.D. Gordon; Dame Pearlette Louisy, governor general of St Lucia; and Dr Kenny Antony, the prime minister. The students performed pieces of Walcott's work, as well as a skit titled "Twavay Derek" (Derek's Work?).

At the opening of Walcott House, Derek asked the gathering to observe a minute's silence in memory of Roddy. Overcome by the emotion, he was unable to read a poem, "The Trusted House", that he had written for the occasion. Robert Lee read it for him. He had celebrated the house, and his mother, long before, in chapter 2 of *Another Life*: "Old house, old woman, old room, / old planes, old buckling membranes of the womb."

CHAPTER SIX

Some time after the Walcotts vacated it, the house was occupied by a printery. In 2005 it was acquired by the Government of St Lucia, which later handed it over to the St Lucia National Trust, to be refurbished and preserved as part of the island's cultural heritage. No doubt the title "The Trusted House" involves a punning reference to this trust, especially since the poem's opening phrase gives "trusted" an initial capital: "The Trusted house". Speakers at the ceremony included the governor general and the prime minister. The latter called attention to the fact that Walcott House was the first stage in the planned development of the area, with the construction of a larger museum block with a cafe, bookshop and courtyard to follow. Glyn Maxwell, who was visiting with Derek and Sigrid for Nobel Laureate Week, also spoke, telling of his experience as Walcott's student at Boston University.

Unfortunately, on 31 May 2017, the St Lucia National Trust found it necessary to issue a press release to the effect that Walcott House would be closed from that day, and for the time being, because of a lack of funding.

From a St Lucian perspective, the culmination of the sequence of celebrations of his career was to occur on 28 February, when the Government of St Lucia inaugurated the national honour of Knight/Dame Commander of St Lucia, and Walcott was one of the first three recipients. He was presented with the award by the governor general. This was now the country's highest national honour, out-topping the St Lucia Cross, which Walcott had been awarded in 1993.

In 2013, in his eighty-fourth year, Walcott suffered a stroke (referred to earlier in this chapter) that was to have a lasting effect on the remainder of his life, leaving him dependent on a wheelchair. It occurred in the middle of a small whirlwind tour. Early in March, he did a reading and an onstage discussion with Seamus Heaney in Boston, for the Association of Writers and Writing Programmes. The discussion was chaired by Rosanna Warren. Derek and Sigrid then rented a car and drove to Oneonta, New York, where he did a reading at Hartwick College on 11 March. This was part of Hartwick's 2012–2013 series of readings by "Four Writers Who Changed the World". After two nights in Oneonta, they drove back to Boston, in freezing cold, to catch a flight to St Lucia. Shortly after arriving back home, he suffered the stroke. This meant that he was unable to go to Munster, Germany, to receive, on 26 May, the Munster Prize for International Poetry. The prize was for *White Egrets*, and the prize money, fifteen thousand and five hundred euros, was shared equally between the poet and the book's translator, Werner von Koppenfels. He was also unable to attend the Hay Festival in Xalapa, Mexico, in October, where he was billed to read; instead, Ida Does's documentary film on him, *Poetry Is an Island*, was shown.

On 5 March 2014, Margaret, Walcott's second wife, died, aged eighty-two. At her memorial service, at the Church of the Assumption, Long Circular Road, Maraval, Derek and Sigrid were present. There was no eulogy, nor any tribute. Jackie Hinkson read Derek's poem "The Season of Phantasmal Peace". In November 2016, Leonard St Hill, Derek's brother-in-law, died in Barbados, where he had served as chief town planner before his retirement. He had been one of the earliest members of the St Lucia Arts Guild.

The years continued to wind down, but Walcott's creativity still flourished. In late 2016, *Morning, Paramin*, by Walcott and Peter Doig, was published in London (Faber and Faber), New York (Farrar, Straus and Giroux), and, under the title *Paramin*, in Paris (Actes Sud), the poems translated into French by Pierre Vinclair. This collaboration between Walcott and Scottish artist Doig who had settled in Trinidad in 2002, has paintings and poems on facing pages, with the poems usually speaking to the paintings. Paramin is a beautiful village in the hills overlooking Trinidad's popular Maracas Bay. Margaret had for a time been a social worker in Paramin. She is remembered in a few of the poems, for example, "In the Heart of Old San Juan", which is virtually an elegy to her.

Walcott and Doig were both present at the launch of the book at the Yard Bookstore in Gros Islet, St Lucia, on 17 December 2016. At the end of the function, Walcott had to be rushed to hospital. It was feared that he had had a heart attack. It turned out to have been a case of low blood sugar, and he did not have to remain in hospital. However, his health steadily deteriorated. The pulmonary disorder from which he had been suffering for some time, necessitated oxygen being always at the ready. On Christmas morning he fell out of bed and broke a femur, consequently needing surgery. Then there was kidney failure, necessitating renal dialysis. He died at home on 17 March 2017, and was accorded a state funeral. The service was held at the cathedral in Castries on 25 March, and he was buried on the Morne, close to the island's other Nobel laureate, Sir Arthur Lewis, and to the memorial monument for the Royal Inniskilling Fusiliers, the Fighting Fifth, about whom he had written in *Another Life*.

※

When Walcott stopped teaching at Boston University in 2007, he was working on the essay "Down the Coast", a reflection on his decades-long effort to make a movie version of *Ti-Jean and His Brothers*. If the film had been completed, he saw the essay serving as a preface to it. However, he subsequently came to see it as "the preservation of the memory of an ambition, a prolonged dream".[34] Through the distinctive capacity of the medium, the film would have realized, more than the play could do, the character of the place, the St Lucian countryside and landscape, and of the people who are grounded in that setting. It would have been Walcott's summary coming-home-again, another interface of location and identity, with the regrounding deepened by the inseparable awareness of all the other locations that have driven his creative imagination. The essay may be read as comprehending, whether explicitly or by implication, virtually all the subjects that Walcott's writing has traversed. To this extent, it is a rounding-off of the "ambition", "the prolonged dream" of his life.

NOTES

1. In *What the Twilight Says*, 87. This and all books by Walcott are hereafter cited in the text using short titles.
2. Roderick Walcott, "In Good Company", *Crusader*, 11 March 2000, 6.
3. "The Land of Look Behind", *Money Index*, 27 April 1993, 24D.
4. Ibid.
5. See "Erika J. Waters (*The Caribbean Writer*) interviews John Figueroa", in *At Home the Green Remains: Caribbean Writing in Honour of John Figueroa*, ed. Esther Figueroa (Kingston: *Caribbean Quarterly*, 2003): 66–74.
6. In conversation with Edward Baugh, Port of Spain, Trinidad and Tobago, 5 May 1975.
7. See Sherlock and Nettleford, *University*, 83.
8. Ibid., 65.
9. Barbara Gloudon, "Go Deh . . . You-Wee", *Sunday Gleaner Magazine*, 7 May 1989, 11.
10. Goldstraw, "Reminiscences", 272, 274.
11. In Baer, *Conversations*, 56.
12. In Collier, *Derek Walcott*, 1:108.
13. Raoul Pantin, "The Trinidad Years", *BWee Caribbean Beat*, Spring 1993, 50.
14. In an email to Edward Baugh, 19 September 2016.
15. In a telephone conversation with Edward Baugh, 24 July 2016.
16. Jeremy Taylor, "The Books and the Sea", *Caribbean Beat*, Spring 1993, 41.

17. See "Derek Walcott", *Bomb*, no. 40 (1992): 46.
18. Seamus Heaney, "The Language of Exile", *Parnassus: Poetry in Review* 8, no. 1 (Fall–Winter 1979): 5–11.
19. In Baer, *Conversations*, 119.
20. Thompson, *Take My Word*, 210.
21. See *Agenda*, special issue on Derek Walcott, 39, nos. 1–3 (2002–2003): 114.
22. See John F. Burns, "Poetic Justice: Briton Quits Post, Saying She Helped Taint a Rival", *New York Times*, 25 May 2009, A1.
23. See Catherine Bennett, "This Spiteful Campaign Has Neither Rhyme nor Reason", *Guardian*, 17 May 2009. https://www.theguardian.com/commentisfree/2009/may/17/derek-walcott-poet-sexual-harassment.
24. James Atlas, "Derek Walcott: Poet of Two Worlds", *New York Times Magazine*, 23 May 1982. http://www.nytimes.com/1982/05/23/magazine/derek-walcott-poet-of-two-worlds-james-atlas.html.
25. Sharon Leach, "A Fine Night of Caribbean Poetry from a Master", *Jamaica Observer*, 28 April 2004, 24.
26. For a substantial summary of the plot, see King, *Derek Walcott*, 412–13.
27. Jean Antoine-Dunne, "Time and Space in Their Indissoluble Connection: Towards an Audio-Visual Caribbean Aesthetic", in "The Montage Principle: Eisenstein in New Cultural and Critical Contexts", edited by Jean Antoine-Dunne with Paula Quigley, *Critical Studies* 21, no. 1 (2003): 125–52. Her *Derek Walcott's Love Affair with Film* is to be published in 2017.
28. See *Epiphany* (Winter–Spring 2007–2008): 157–90.
29. See *Kunapipi* 11, no. 1 (1989): 138–42.
30. See David Streitfeld, "Derek Walcott Becomes First Caribbean Writer to Receive Nobel Prize", *International Herald Tribune*, 9 October 1992, 1. (The Guadeloupean-born Saint-John Perse had won the prize in 1960, but by then was thought of mostly as a French poet.)

NOTES

31. See Geordie Greig, "On the Crest of a Wave", *Sunday Times*, 14 February 1999, 8.
32. Jason Sifflet, "The Wrath of Walcott", part 4, *Star*, 25 July 2005, 8.
33. See J.D. Douglas, "Omeros . . . What a Circus!", *Voice* (St Lucia), 3 May 2016, http://thevoiceslu.com/2016/05/omeros-what-a-circus/.
34. Walcott, "Down the Coast", 190.

BIBLIOGRAPHY

Bruce King's comprehensive *Derek Walcott: A Caribbean Life* (Oxford: Oxford University Press, 2000), the first book-length biography of Walcott, is an invaluable mine of information. An important complement to this work in respect of biography is King's *Derek Walcott and West Indian Drama* (Oxford: Oxford University Press, 1995).

Two crucial autobiographical essays by Walcott, one from early in his career, the other from late, are "Leaving School" (in Robert Hamner, ed., *Critical Perspectives on Derek Walcott* [Boulder: Lynne Rienner, 1997]) and "Down the Coast" (in *Epiphany* [Winter–Spring 2007–2008]). Another valuable source of biographical information is William Baer's edition of Walcott interviews (*Conversations with Derek Walcott* [Jackson: University Press of Mississippi, 1996]). Then there is Irma E. Goldstraw's *Derek Walcott: An Annotated Bibliography of His Works* (New York: Garland, 1984).

Sizeable collections of Walcott papers, including manuscripts and correspondence, are housed in the Thomas Fisher Rare Book Library, University of Toronto, and the Alma Jordan Library, University of the West Indies, St Augustine. There is a relatively small collection in the library at the University of the West Indies, Mona, including the holograph, unpublished prose work "Another Life", from which the autobiographical poem *Another Life* developed.

BIBLIOGRAPHY

Only those works by Walcott actually quoted in the text appear in the bibliography below.

Baer, William, ed. *Conversations with Derek Walcott.* Jackson: University Press of Mississippi, 1996.

Collier, Gordon, ed. *Derek Walcott: The Journeyman Years.* 2 vols. Amsterdam: Rodopi, 2013.

King, Bruce. *Derek Walcott: A Caribbean Life.* Oxford: Oxford University Press, 2000.

Sherlock, Philip, and Rex Nettleford. *The University of the West Indies: A Caribbean Response to the Challenge of Change.* London: Macmillan, 1990.

Goldstraw, Lawrence. "Reminiscences of Derek Walcott and the Trinidad Theatre Workshop". In *Critical Perspectives on Derek Walcott*, edited by Robert D. Hamner, 272–77. Boulder: Lynne Rienner, 1997.

Thompson, Ralph. *Take My Word for It: A Jamaican Memoir.* Leeds: Peepal Tree, 2016.

Walcott, Derek. *The Arkansas Testament.* New York: Farrar, Straus and Giroux, 1987.

———. *The Bounty.* New York: Farrar, Straus and Giroux, 1997.

———. "Down the Coast". *Epiphany* (Winter–Spring 2007–2008): 157–90.

———. *The Fortunate Traveller.* New York: Farrar, Straus and Giroux, 1981.

———. *In a Green Night.* London: Cape, 1962.

———. *The Gulf and Other Poems.* London: Cape, 1969.

———. *The Haitian Trilogy.* New York: Farrar, Straus and Giroux, 2002.

———. *Midsummer.* London: Faber, 1984.

———. *The Prodigal.* New York: Farrar, Straus and Giroux, 2004.

———. *Sea Grapes.* New York: Farrar, Straus and Giroux, 1976.

BIBLIOGRAPHY

———. *The Star-Apple Kingdom*. New York: Farrar, Straus and Giroux, 1979.
———. *Tiepolo's Hound*. New York: Farrar, Straus and Giroux, 2000.
———. *What the Twilight Says*. New York: Farrar, Straus and Giroux, 1998.
———. *White Egrets*. New York: Farrar, Straus and Giroux, 2010.

ACKNOWLEDGEMENTS

I am grateful to Sigrid Nama, Elizabeth Walcott Hackshaw, Anna Walcott Hardy, Robert Lee, Laurence Breiner, Ronan Noone and Kate Snodgrass for their assistance with information, and to Mervyn Morris for his careful and valuable comments on the draft manuscript.

CPSIA information can be obtained
at www.ICGtesting.com
Printed in the USA
LVHW11s1730031018
592282LV00001B/2/P